NEWMARKET

THE

B.B.A.

JUBILEE

HANDICAP

WEDNESDAY 7th JULY 1971

WITHOUT RESERVE

Some Recollections of a
Bloodstock Agent

WITHOUT RESERVE

*Some Recollections of a
Bloodstock Agent*

Robin Hastings

Foreword by John Hislop

J. A. ALLEN

London

First published in Great Britain by
J A Allen & Co Ltd
1 Lower Grosvenor Place
London SWIW OEL
1987

British Library Cataloguing in Publication Data

Hastings, Robin
  Without reserve: some recollections of
  a bloodstock agent.
  1. Hastings, Robin   2. Horsemen and
  horsewomen—Great Britain—Biography
  I. Title
  636.1′2′0924   SF284.52.H3/

  ISBN 0-85131-455-4

Phototypeset in 13pt Bembo
by Charles Skilton Ltd
Balmoral Publishing Works, Cheddar
Printed and bound by Charles Clarke Printers Ltd
Haywards Heath, Sussex

To my wife, Jean

BY THE SAME AUTHOR

The Rifle Brigade 1939-45

Photograph Acknowledgements

Plates 6/7 H. B. Mason. Plate 8 Daily Graphic.
Plate 12 Fotonews. Plates 12/14/16 Sport and General.
Plate 18 Lesley Sampson.
Plate 10, jacket illustration and endpaper illustrations reproduced by
generous permission of Peter Biegel.

Contents

List of Photographs

1. Robin and Jean Hastings at Mexico City Racecourse in 1955.

2. Robin on his first pony "Polly" with his father, the Hon. Osmond Hastings.

3. Robin aged 8 at his Gloucestershire home.

4. Robin out hunting with the North Cotswold in 1938.

5. Robin at Stratford-upon-Avon on Chatmo beating Bryan Marshall and P. J. Doyle in 1948.

6. Robin at the last hurdle at Doncaster before winning on Eight Reigns in 1948.

7. Mr. A. V. Tabor (bowler hat) about to lead in Eight Reigns.

8. Robin winning at Leicester on Monk's Crest in 1950 from Colonel Billy Smith — first ride after broken collarbone.

9. Jean Hastings and Rupert in 1951 — two reasons for leaving the army.

10. Merry Madcap (Lester Piggott up) at Salisbury in 1964 by Peter Biegel.

11. Mrs Scott and her dogs.

12. The late Danny Van Clief's Unbiased with Geoffrey Brooke and Doug Smith.

13. Never Too Late winning the 1960 Oaks from Paimpont and Imberline.

14. Nasram II winning the 1964 King George VI and Queen Elizabeth Diamond Stakes at Ascot from the Derby winner Santa Claus.

Foreword

I first met Robin Hastings shortly after the war. His name was familiar as a distinguished soldier, the youngest battalion commander during those years, who had won the DSO (and bar), OBE and MC, but our military paths had not crossed and our first encounter was on Charlie Stalker's bench in the jockeys' changing room. Robin and I came under Charlie's care through similar channels; he through Gerry Hardy, who trained a horse for him and was valeted in his riding days by Charlie; I through Jack Reardon, a trainer for whom I had my first, and nearly last, ride, and whose jockey Gerry Hardy had been.

Robin was then a "claimer," but had shown that he had ability, so when George Todd asked me to find him a jockey for a bumper race at Salisbury I put Robin in for the ride. While in such circumstances the first thought is to recommend someone from the same bench, all who knew George Todd will appreciate that to supply him with anyone but a competent rider would have had grave repercussions. My judgment was vindicated: the horse won. The story had its funny side, as the author relates.

The account of Robin's riding days is told with wit and modesty and will bring back memories to all who have experienced the vicissitudes of riding under National Hunt Rules.

The bulk of the book concerns the author's life as a bloodstock agent, and later as Chairman of the British Bloodstock Agency. I cannot recall a book about this profession, so it it interesting to find one explaining how the business works and what it entails. On the face of it, it may sound a pleasant, exciting life, with a fair measure of what used to be termed in the Army "Good Time Charlies," that is to say, jaunts at the employer's expense. In fact it entails hard work, business acumen, knowledge of all aspects of the thoroughbred and of pedigrees, diplomacy, bottomless stamina, a constitution able to overcome difficulties peculiar to foreign parts and to withstand the unavoidable excesses of good living, not to mention the most important quality of all: a flair for the profession. Not a few agents and agencies fail to survive.

The reader will find this life fully and fascinatingly described, learning practical lessons about buying, selling and assessing horses, their idiosyncracies and those of clients, and something of tourism in the world of thoroughbreds.

The BAA is the oldest and most famous of all bloodstock agencies, and the prominent position of British thorough-breds in the world's market over the years is due chiefly to its work: "We (the French) cannot compete with you in the bloodstock market; wherever you go, there is Colonel Hastings," M. Jean Romanet once remarked to me. I am old enough to have known the founders of the Agency: E.E. Coussel, who gave and inscribed for me the split-pedigree book I still use; Jock Crawford, the veterinary director; Brigadier Scott, a contemporary of my Father's in the Indian Cavalry; all legendary names in the profession.

The story is not just an account of successful deals. With refreshing candour the author also refers to expensive failures, which are an unavoidable factor in the business. Nevertheless, prospective buyers of bloodstock can take heart from the number of the author's cheap acquisitions which have turned out to be good horses.

References to happy days out hunting and with rod and gun, sometimes in distant lands, made enjoyable inroads into the text, as do descriptions of the scenery and environment in different parts of the world. I am sure that this book will do well for the author as so many of his purchases have done for clients of the BBA.

JOHN HISLOP

Introduction

This book is not intended as an autobiography, for I have many interests other than those described. Nor is it a history of the British Bloodstock Agency for it does scant justice to my partners' considerable efforts. It is not intended to inform nor to instruct but merely to provide a little quiet entertainment for those interested in racing and breeding over the last fifty years.

I am deeply indebted to Bill Curling whose idea it was that something should be written and who has slaved as a true professional to keep an amateur's effort on the rails. I am also indebted to my secretary, Jackie Rich, who has battled with an illegible handwriting to some effect and to the BBA Pedigree Department for some factual assistance. And, of course, to my wife Jean, who has done her best not to interrupt me when I am trying to write.

I apologise to those who now make the BBA go — Michael Wates, Christo Philipson, Brian Gething, Philip Payne-Gallwey, Charles Smith-Bingham, Johnnie Lewis, Joss Collins, James Marshall, John Harvey-Barnes and Simon Morley for hardly mentioning them — for this is my story, not that of the BBA; nor must I forget Sonia and Cyril Brown, who run Byculla, the BBA house at Newmarket, and who have acquired many grateful friends from all over the world in the last twenty years.

CHAPTER 1

Early Days

WHEN BILL CURLING SUGGESTED that I should write what amounted to some extracts from my racing memories, I thought that there was nothing serious which I could contribute to what has already been said and written by and for jockeys, trainers and racehorse owners. If I did put pen to paper, it would have to concern a few personal experiences on the turf. It would be for him to judge not of their importance but of their interest to outsiders.

You do not land yourself a job with the British Bloodstock Agency without some racing background so I will explain for a moment the two threads which run through my early life and inclined me to opening the last pages of the daily papers first.

My grandfather, the then Lord Huntingdon, lived in Ireland in the Midlands at a house with the romantic name of Sharavogue. There, like his father before him, he hunted the Ormonde Hounds, and for several seasons the East Galway, as well as the Harriers on Sundays. What he did in the summers is not recorded. Her Ladyship bore him a large number of children and wrote charming short stories and fairy tales in the Celtic manner.

The organisation of the family was directed by the butler, a gentleman of whom I have seen photographs, showing a fine pair of mutton chop whiskers. He looked after the children, ran the household and kept at bay the local tradesmen, who frequently appeared to demand payment of their bills. If the truth be told, there seems to have been very little money to maintain either family or hounds.

None of the children went to school and their education was left to such tutors and governesses as did not offend the butler himself. He did not do a bad job on the boys; the eldest

1

became one of the best amateur huntsmen of the time, the second hunted, shot and played polo with the best and the youngest trained four winners of the Grand National, one of which he rode himself.

When the children had grown up, they were despatched to their cousin, the then Duchess of Newcastle, with instructions to find husbands or wives able to keep them. Most of them did.

My father married a Highland lady and they returned to Ireland to lease Gowran Castle, where the racecourse now stands, but then the property of Lord Annaly. My Uncle Aubrey lived with them. Between them my father and uncle played polo, shot snipe and hunted, until my mother counted sixty horses, polo ponies, hunters, hacks and carriage horses on the place. She then thought it wiser to move to England and in Rendcomb, a village near Cirencester, a house was found, where there was hunting and two polo grounds but not so many snipe. Uncle Aubrey went with them.

Uncle Aubrey suffered from one severe disadvantage. When he was a small boy, he was sharpening a stick, no doubt to make a rabbit-snare, when the knife slipped and went into his eye. As a result he lost the sight of that eye for ever and was forbidden by the doctors to learn to read and write. Thus at the age when most people were about to take on a job in life, he was at a great disadvantage. My mother being a Scottish lady of some determination insisted that he should learn to be literate.

Freddie Maxwell, the former Lambourn trainer, who came from near Sharavogue knew the family well and remembers going in a railway carriage with Uncle Aubrey, then grown up, seeing him try to read one of those books which proclaimed " A " is for apple, " B " for butcher etc., which were popular at a time when it was thought proper for children to learn to read. But the real ace served by my mother was to produce *The Horse Veterinary Dictionary* in nine volumes, which Uncle Aubrey was determined to read. Armed with this knowledge he set up as a trainer with two horses on the other side of the road to Rendcomb. He was soon to move to Wroughton and fame.

I was, of course, thrilled to have so famous a relation. At my preparatory school, I followed the Wroughton horses with a keen intensity. One of the masters, Mr. Pembroke, used to take The Sporting Chronicle and let me have a look at it when I should have been mugging up latin verbs. I suppose he hoped for information of which I was totally devoid.

Both Uncle Aubrey and my father died comparatively young. But I remember going over to Wroughton several times with my father. Once a beautifully made un-named four-year-old was led out, a bay with black points. My father thought he was the best-looking horse he had ever seen. He was named Kellsborough Jack and earned more than his share of glory at Aintree and Cheltenham, winning the Grand National in 1933.

Another time we were shown an un-named gelding belonging to Mr. Hugh Lloyd Thomas of the Foreign Office. As the door of the box was opened the horse stepped forward and the owner, being a perfect diplomat, stepped to one side. The whole of the staff and visitors were soon engaged in combing the village streets to find the horse, who under the name of Royal Mail was to become a famous steeplechaser and to win the Grand National in 1937.

There was also, of course, Brown Jack, one of the greatest characters of all time. I am told that when my uncle went over to buy him, he was shown a gaggle of young horses in a rough uneven field, covered in rocks and gorse bushes. They galloped round and down a steep hill. He picked out two as exceptional movers down hill. One was Brown Jack, for whom he found an owner in Sir Harold Wernher and the other for whom he could not find a buyer at what was then considered the high price of £600 was Arctic Star, who was to win the Cesarewitch of 1928.

When I left my preparatory school and the use of Mr. Pembroke's *Sporting Chronicle* — I was due, like my brother, to go to Mr. Chitty's house at Eton. My brother had not been very happy there, nor was my mother very happy with Eton in general. However, I was hauled up to be seen by the Reverend Chitty. As I was head of my preparatory school, there was little doubt that he would take me into his house. I distinctly remember standing on the doorstep with the Reverend gentleman who intoned "He is just like a little white mouse." This predisposed me against Eton, a view with which the bank manager agreed. So I went to Stowe instead.

It was there that I was playing rugger — not the same game in which my first cousin, Peter Hastings would have played before going on to represent Oxford and England — but rugger all the same! I tripped, or was tripped, and broke my right wrist. As I could not write, I was sent home for three or four weeks.

One of the first neighbours I met in Moreton-in-Marsh was Frank Atherton Brown, a great friend of the family. He was one of the two brothers so well portrayed under another name in Siegfried Sassoon's *Memoirs of a Foxhunting Man*, as setting the Pucklestone (Atherstone) alight. He and his brother Harry were top-class riders. They were as good as most professionals, if not better. Frank was supposed to be the better over hurdles and Harry over fences. But they lived a wild life and went through the considerable fortunes they had inherited.

By the time I knew him Frank was living at Bourton-on-the-Hill and training some twenty to twenty-five jumpers. When he saw me with my arm in a sling he immediately offered to take me racing. From the time I was laid up while my wrist was mending and all the school holidays thereafter, I was taken racing by him and began to learn at least the language employed by those who rode and trained on the journeys to and from the racecourse.

Riding for him at the time were Eric Foster and Billy Speck, both leading jump jockeys in their time. Later on came Gerry Wilson, winner of the 1934 Grand National on Golden Miller, and Geoffrey (later Sir Geoffrey) Shakerley, who had considerable success on his own horses. I would see the horses work, hear what he was going to tell the jockey to

4

do on the journey home, hear the race and the future of the horses discussed. I listened — I do not know if I learnt!

One of the highlights of my journeys with Frank was to Liverpool, when he was running in the National D'Eyncourt, runner up in the Lancashire Chase of 1935 to the National winner Cooleen. The then Clerk of the course, Sir Crocker Bulteel kindly took me round the course and I was suitably amazed at the size of the fences. It was Reynoldstown's second year (1936) and I watched Fulke Walwyn win on him. But sadly D'Eyncourt fell at the other end of the course and broke his neck. So the horsebox went home empty.

Frank Brown was a man of great kindness and great wit. Despite his terrible falls racing and hunting, he remained a great companion to young and old. He was also a thoughtful trainer and would try harder than most with moderate or ungenuine horses. I remember one horse who would stop on the gallops or in a race at the slightest provocation. He would tell the lad to jump him off and remain in front. The lad on the other horse would be told to remain a neck behind throughout. Provided he did this the old horse worked well but if anyone went past him or dropped well behind, he would pack it up. Unfortunately you could not give the same orders in a race!

When I had finished my time at Stowe, the Headmaster, the great J.F. Roxburgh suggested that, as I had no particular career in view, I should go to Oxford. Christ Church was chosen — not because my grandfather had been sent down for driving a coach and horses round Tom Quad with the future King Edward VII on board but because my mother's relations had been there. I did my three years there on the handsome sum of £300 a year, out of which I had to pay my "battels" (university and college dues) and was able to keep a horse and a car.

Unfortunately, instead of getting my head down to work at Oxford I became one of the Bullingdon boys and spent my time beagling, hunting, shooting and, I am afraid, drinking.

My father's youngest sister was married to Sir William Bass, a former well-known master of the Meynell Hounds in

5

the 1930's and a man of considerable fortune. But they had no children. Uncle Billie was known to be looking round for a suitable recipient of his wealth when he died. Lady Noreen on the other hand felt it her duty to find some respectable girl possessed of a fortune to match up with her impecunious Oxford University nephew.

In those days they raced at Derby and indeed had a fashionable three days meeting in the autumn, where one race a day was worth £1,000 or £890 to the winner — big stuff in the 1930's.

The big houses in the Meynell country always held large houseparties for the race meeting. I stayed once or twice at Lady Burton's at Rangemore where we dined off gold plate but I was more often at Byrkley with my uncle and my aunt Noreen. There were usually present some fifteen or twenty regular race goers, expert in eating and skilful at bridge and one or two very eligible young ladies for my benefit. In the case of the latter, their fortunes were invariably more attractive than their faces. They regarded me as of no consequence — a penniless and undeveloped schoolboy !

It so happened that one year at the time of the Derby Autumn meeting, I was one of the houseparty, composed as expected. Arthur Portman of *Horse and Hound* and the gambler Jack Clayton are two I can remember. Jack Clayton was owner of the stable at Newmarket where Norman Bertie trained the Derby winner Pinza.

Aunt Noreen, having given up hunting due to being over-faced with under-exercised and over-fed horses, had been given a pony by Hughie Lonsdale (the Yellow Earl) from his Lake District estates to ride about the place. It had just arrived and had been subjected to a week of Byrkley treatment — lots of food and no exercise.

It was led out for me to try by the old stud groom himself, who clearly was subjected to the same regime as his horses. His stomach was so large that his belt would not go round his middle part and hung as it were at half-mast half way down his trousers. The house-party lined the steps of the house as if for a photograph. The pony, a good looking tit, was led

6

through the iron gate into the park and I was hoisted on board for the trial run. As soon as he had put me up, the old groom let go of the iron gate which slammed shut with a resounding clash. The pony leapt sideways in the air and swept me off like Absalom on the branches of a nearby tree. As it galloped off into the park, the house party on the steps slowly dissolved and what little hope I might have had of inheriting Uncle Billie's millions disappeared into the distance with Lord Lonsdale's pony. I doubt if Peter Hastings was subjected to any such equestrian test!

Meanwhile, in spite of my misfortune on the Lonsdale pony I had a few rides in public. After being third in a good class handicap at Newbury which I suppose I should have won by ten lengths, I went to Taunton to ride in a novices hurdle. In a pile up on the far side, the horse Antic broke his neck and I was removed to Taunton Hospital with a fractured skull. This was my last year at Oxford and as it turned out it had its advantages. First of all I had a convalescence at Bishops Liddiard with Stephen Vernon's parents — a lovely home. Then the doctors told me that I could return to Oxford, provided I did not work too hard.

It was an almost perfect position for someone taking their schools in two months time. However, I did do some work and felt that I had done reasonably well despite, at one time, taking benzedrine as a stimulant and writing the same word twelve times. Sometime after the schools, I was sent for by the examiner for a "viva" or verbal examination. By that time I would have been better able to answer questions about what was second in the selling hurdle at Plumpton than about Wolsey and the monasteries or Peel and the Corn Laws. However, the gentlemen listened politely and I imagined that they were deciding whether to give me either nothing or a fourth — that degree set aside for indolent sons of vice-chancellors, relations of foreign royalty and those who have fallen on their heads in the last term. Imagine my surprise when I picked up *The Times* one day to see that I had a second-class degree in Modern History and the totally useless entitlement to put BA after my name!

If I had been given a First, it would have made the whole difference to my life, most of which would have been spent with my nose full of dust from the shelves of the Bodleian or walking along the two path with muffler and pipe, being surrounded by dons who waved the Red Flag in their left hand and demanded that the steward placed another glass of the '21 in their right hand. If I had got my First, Mrs. Thatcher might even have anticipated one vote for her Fellowship.

As it was I was left with no definite ideas about a profession and was persuaded by my tutor to stay on for a year to read law. But even to a Bullingdon boy, it was clear that war was very much in the offing. I was an officer in the University O.T.C. The present Duke of Norfolk, Neville (now Lord) Wigram and Humphrey (now Sir Humphrey) Prideaux were the others. It seemed sensible to try to get into a regiment where one would be with friends rather than wait to be called up as a private in the Intelligence Corps.

My family knew little about the army but were assured that I could not afford to go into a cavalry regiment. My father had known Sir Reginald Seymour, who recommended the 60th (K.R.R.C.) Rifles. Both battalions of that regiment were abroad and so I was sent for my attachment to the first battalion of the sister regiment, The Rifle Brigade. For quite unmilitary reasons the Rifle Brigade decided to pinch me and so, as it was all the same to me, I left the two regiments to sort it out.

At the beginning of 1939 I was a subaltern in the Rifle Brigade stationed at Tidworth — and, more to the point, had arranged to be second jockey to ride Kim Muir's light-weights. That officer had purchased a training stable near Tidworth and had set up there his private trainer. Muir was to go well on Away in Bogskar's National in 1940 but sadly he did not survive the war.

From my point of view just as things were settling down well at home, though looking grim internationally, the blow fell. I was told that I had been posted to the second battalion in India. I knew so little about the army that I had not anticipated exile of this sort. In those days it was sometimes possible to pay someone else to go instead of you. But I had not the resources for this ploy and in any case could not find anyone willing to go. If I had stayed at Tidworth I might have ridden a winner but I should certainly have gone to Calais and ended up either dead or a prisoner of war.

As it was, I made the most of my last days in England. Of the fourteen days left, two were Sundays, one day had to be wasted going to the War Office and on the other eleven I went hunting! On the very last day — 25th February 1939 — I started the day by riding unsuccessfully in the regimental cross-country race in the V.W.H. country, then drove to a meet at Bradwell Grove, at the home of the Heyworth family, and had a day's hunting with the Heythrop. Finally I set off with the old chauffeur to motor to Southampton, where a boat, full of soldiers waiting to be seasick, was ready to take me to Bombay. It was to be three years and more before I saw England again.

CHAPTER 2

Apricot and Company

AFTER SIX YEARS of war I was eventually posted back to England as an Instructor at the Staff College at Camberley in Surrey. This is a job which usually results in grey hairs and nervous breakdowns rather than in riding winners. But with the war only just over we had a pretty good knowledge of what a division consisted of and most of the early students were senior officers who had just missed a staff course. Among my particular lot was Moshe Dyan who was a future commander-in-chief of the Israeli Army and General Baig, future Commander in Chief of the Pakistani Army. I was therefore able to have more time off than is usual in such a job.

I thought I might start riding again and looked around for something to buy. In my search I went to the Lillington Stud near Leamington Spa in Warwickshire. The owner, Sidney McGregor, was well-known as the part owner with the actor Tom Walls of April the Fifth, the 1932 Derby winner. Not successful as a sire of flat race horses, April the Fifth had some good results when mated with Mr. McGregor's jumping mares. From a whole field of little April's I chose a four-year-old bay mare broken and ridden but not, they said, tried. She was big enough to go hurdling but hardly a steeple-chasing type. I bought her for £150.

The next thing was to find a trainer. Epsom seemed the nearest large training centre to the Staff College at Camberley. I was recommended to ask Gerry Hardy, if he would take her. He had been an absolutely first class National Hunt jockey until he broke his leg at Plumpton. He was disgracefully treated both on the course and in hospital and ended up with a useless and extremely painful leg. This inclined him to drown the pain in the usual way. One of his

10

stratagems was to pour out half a cup of tea and fill the rest with rum, oblivious of the fact that the smell of rum filled the room!

When I met Gerry he had a stable at Epsom, training jumpers, but with some flat race horses as well. The best I suppose of the flat racers at that time was Avignon, a marvellous ride at home, who won the 1947 Chesterfield Cup at Goodwood amongst other races. Of the steeplechasers Black Jennifer, oddly enough a gelding, who won a fair few steeplechases and ran in Caughoo's 1947 National. Riding for Hardy were Jimmy Hickey, flat and hurdles and E.C. "Taffy" Taylor, hurdles and fences. It was, of course, a betting stable — as on the basis of stake money at the time it had to be. But it was not one which could afford the luxury of keeping a horse for six months. They had to do their best when they were well. Gerry was adept at knowing when this was so, without the modern day assistance of blood tests, weighing machines and twenty-four hour veterinary care. He would watch them walking round for a few minutes when they came out in the morning and pick out by eye those really ready to run.

To my surprise he agreed to accept Apricot, my mare. This was probably because he enjoyed the idea of getting his own back on a Colonel, after his years of National Service! She went down to Epsom and he seemed quite pleased with her except for one thing — she really knew how to pull. So I could never ride her in strong work.

When Apricot had been there a few months, Charlie Smirke came over to ride something which was due for a run on the flat. After he had worked this horse, Gerry said to Smirke: "Charlie, jump on this mare and see if she is any good. She belongs to a blinking soldier. Just watch her, she takes a bit of a hold."

It was a foggy morning and only one strip of the gallop was open. The gallops on either side were marked off with iron chains at intervals. Charlie had not really listened to Gerry's warning and so he kicked her in the ribs and was gone at full speed straight away. But instead of keeping to the gallop she

11

swerved to the left and thought it more fun to go up the closed gallop, jumping the chains! She disappeared into the fog with Gerry roaring with laughter — not so funny for the owner who anticipated having to pick up the bits in Stanley Wootton's garden. After quite some time Charlie Smirke returned. All he said was "some amateur's ride!"

Nevertheless, in a race Apricot was a good ride and gave me much fun that season of 1946-1947. Finally at the beginning of April on Easter Monday she won a novice hurdle at the West Norfolk Hunt Meeting at Fakenham — my first winner.

Gerry got her ready early the next season and I finished second on her in a handicap hurdle at Fontwell in September before taking her north for a handicap hurdle at Market Rasen, which he was sure she would win. Because of his painful leg he did not go all the way up to Lincolnshire, but left me to my own devices.

I thought, if you could call it thinking, that if I jumped off she would probably run away for $1\frac{1}{2}$ miles and then something would come and "do" her. So I planned to "lob" out of the gate and get a lead. Of course, I overdid it and when the gate went up, we were left five to ten lengths. Although she did make up some ground, she could only manage third place.

I left before the last race and had the misfortune to stop at some traffic lights, next door to the car in which the steward's secretary, Colonel Miles Thompson, was travelling, also before the last race. Someone in our car — and I hope it was not me — yelled "If we had known you were going early, we could have pulled one up in the last!"

The next day, being Sunday, I had to go over to Epsom and face the music. Gerry could not understand how she had been beaten. When I said that I did not get away very well, he rang round Lincolnshire to find someone who had seen the race, finally getting confirmation of my story. So we went out to see her and there she was "having a pick of grass" with her lad, Edgar Springate. She looked so well that Gerry said "She is in at Plumpton tomorrow. Why not run her?" There were no four-day declarations in those days.

So I hurried back to the staff college to find someone to do my work. Luckily one of the instructors was Jack Masters, soon to be famous as the author of *Bhowani Junction* and all those marvellous books about India. He had nothing to do on a Monday in October and agreed to take my syndicate. If any of them attained "P.S.C." (passed Staff College) after their name, they no doubt owed it to his teaching.

Off I went to Plumpton where the whole team were ready to give me my orders. There was a hot favourite trained by Gerry Laurence, who liked a bet. But it was not a great field. For once everything went right. I jumped off fourth or fifth, made up ground down the hill, joined the leader at the last and came away to win.

While I was changing and wondering if I was a cross between the stars of their time — Fred Rees and Bryan Marshall — the stewards' secretary came up. "The Stewards want to see you," he said.

The senior steward was the then Lord Abergavenny, whom I knew slightly, and there were familiar Sussex faces among the others. Their first question was "Did you back your horse today?"

I said I had not.

"Did you back it on Saturday?"

I said "Well I don't bet, but I had a tenner there to go towards presents for the yard if I won."

They then asked the stewards' secretary if there had been any money for the mare. He said the ring inspector told him that there did not appear to have been any.

"How do you explain the difference in running between Saturday and today?"

I told them the story of how I had tried to drop her out and had been left. They also asked the steward's secretary if he had seen the start. He looked up his book and said "Yes, she was slowly away."

To my great relief they said: "Thank you, Colonel Hastings, you can go." Nor did anything about the enquiry appear in the Racing Calendar! Nevertheless, it did me a great deal of good. In the weighing room, the jockeys thought it was the funniest thing for years and I had to put up with a great deal of teasing.

Apricot did me well. She was in the money often and I rode her to another win at Wincanton on Boxing Day 1947, when she beat a bigger and better field than at Fakenham at Easter. But the next year she trained off and although I eventually tried to breed from her she only produced one crooked-legged foal.

There was another officer at the Staff College, a student, David Smyly, who had an old plater which he liked to ride. So as to save a bit in driving, he sent him to Gerry Hardy. He had great fun on him winning chases at various places, including Fakenham. But as a student he did not always find it easy to get off to ride and after the Staff College he had one of those secret jobs, which made it very difficult to get in touch with him.

Gerry got the old horse ready at the beginning of 1948 and entered him up well. But he could not contact the owner. So, after a bit he said "I have got Eastern Lord in at Nottingham next week. You had better ride him." I told him that he had better clear this with the owner. But I do not know if he ever did.

Unfortunately, Nottingham is a very long way from Camberley. Furthermore, I had a syndicate discussion to take on that morning. Luckily, the RAF Instructor, who had by his terms to keep up his flying hours, was often ready to fly me to the races. So there he was waiting at Blackbushe Aerodrome. Unfortunately for me the Assistant Commandant, a gunner, who would not even have known they raced at the Gunner's Course at Larkhill, came in just before I was leaving and made me late.

The first thing the airman said when I got to Blackbushe was "The weather report is very bad. Do you really want to go?" I said I had to and off we went in a small two-seater plane. The forecasters were right and we bumped up and down in a fierce head wind making me air sick and, more important, late. But my friend persevered and contacted the aerodrome where we were due, so that we were met by a smart Air Force car plus driver and corporal.

When I said "Please go to Colwick Park Racecourse," their mouths fell open, but not until they arrived at the gate did I say a word. Then I only said that I had a ride in the first and made a dash for the weighing room. In the race I had been told to lie up, and, if anything came upsides, to give him a kick and he would jump the other down. It did not, of course, turn out that way, as Eastern Lord was a bit slow at the first two. But, gradually moving up, he was there with a chance at the second last, when he hit it hard. Taking care to replace me in the saddle, he set off after the leader, jumped the last superbly and won.

Hardly having time to take in that this was my first steeplechase win, I rushed for the station, this time in a taxi, and leapt into the first first-class carriage I saw. To my horror there was only one other person in it. This was the well-known figure of General Sir Brian Horrocks, G.O.C. Northern Command or something of that sort. He knew me and what my job was. So he immediately started to try to find out what on earth I was doing in Nottingham. I withheld all information until we got to London and carefully kept the racing results portion of the evening paper out of his sight!

In those days there was not the same competition between professionals and amateurs as there is now, nor the same disciplines to prevent sham amateurism. There were many more owner-riders, several soldiers riding regularly and a mass of beginners, most of whom would become professional in due course. As no fee and only a small amount of insurance was levied when an amateur was put up, the jockeys disliked those who rode novice chasers and the like just to save the fee. Quite rightly the jockeys considered this their perquisite.

When you had ridden seven winners you were required to come before the National Hunt Stewards to state your case for a licence, if a jockey, or a permit, if an amateur. My fifth and sixth winners came rather more quickly than expected and I found myself going to Plumpton with three rides, the last of which was that good race-mare Slender, whom I should have loved to have ridden. But her trainer, Ryan Price, quite correctly said that he would not risk being left without a jockey if one of the others won. So I never did ride her.

I asked therefore for an interview with the stewards and was given a date several weeks ahead. This did not suit me at all, as I might by then have been sent abroad by the Army. So, after much lobbying, they very kindly agreed to see me in an interval, in which normally perhaps they would have spent their time comparing the Taylor's '27 with the Cockburn's '19!

On the day before I was due to appear one of the stewards asked me to ride a mare of his first time out at Taunton. He said "Just make certain she sees the hurdles and goes on the outside all the way. If she is going well, give her a kick, but don't hit her. I want her to jump well and enjoy herself." In other words I was to give her a "school." This I duly did. She was no good. The next day I appeared at Weatherby's office and found the owner of the mare sitting on the right of the senior steward, who was Sir Edward Hanmer. The interview went like this.

"You are a regular soldier?"

"Yes."

"And you ride your own horses?"

"Yes," I said thinking of the two very moderate animals I had.

"And those of your friends?"

For a moment I thought of answering "Yes, and those of the members of the National Hunt Committee when they are not off," but contented myself with "Yes."

"All right, Colonel Hastings, you may have your permit." After which they went back to the port. I often wonder what would have happened if I had let one word slip. I expect it would have made no difference for by then they would have been thinking of the port.

I had known Bunty and Arthur Taylor for years, mainly from North Cotswold days. They had the occasional jumper in training, mostly home-bred. One day they came up to me and asked if I would like to ride a mare of theirs called Pongo Lass. Of course I said yes and went off to Towcester on Whit Monday in May, 1948 when she was entered in a Novice Chase. Her trainer, "Ginger" Dennistoun, was there, standing legs apart with an enormous pipe sticking out at a rakish angle from his considerable jaw.

I can remember his orders now: "She will jump the first few fences well and then will hit one really hard and you will fall off" — pause — "If you are still together, kick her along after that."

It worked almost exactly as he said. She jumped the first few and then really hit one. I did not quite fall off and was surprised to find that as we came up the hill, she was staying on well enough to be third. I returned to scale, expecting some rough treatment from the Dennistoun tongue for being so far behind. But, to my surprise, he seemed quite pleased and asked me to ride her the next season.

The first race was at Devon and Exeter, high up on Haldon Moor, a few miles from Exeter. There were about seven runners, one from Newmarket, a hot favourite, and one ridden by Anthony Mildmay. I set off behind and after passing the stands we turned away into the mist. At the first fence after the stands, I saw a tremendous tussle in progress and one horse and rider went sailing out into the heather. I thought no more of it and plugged on, passing Anthony Mildmay at the last but not getting to the Newmarket horse.

Ginger and Arthur were not waiting for me at the unsaddling enclosure and when I went into the weighing room I soon sensed that something was wrong. After a bit, I asked my valet, Charlie Stalker, what was up. He said "They all think you are going to object." At that moment Anthony Mildmay came over.

"Weren't you off?" he said. I said "Yes, of course I was."

"Then why did you not object? The winner missed that fence where the schemozzle took place."

I, of course, was the only person not to see it. By now it was twelve minutes after the race and I rushed out to comb the bars for owner and trainer. But by the time I found their particular bar and "got our act" together, it was too late, the quarter of an hour time limit for objecting was up. Ginger then committed himself to one of the great remarks of his life — which is saying something!

"Will you ride her at Folkestone on Monday week?"

"I will have to see if the army will let me off."

"Why don't you turn professional? You can ride *all* of mine!"

I think he was a bit insulted when I laughed.

That misfortune, was, in fact, a boon, as Pongo Lass remained a maiden and I won three novice chases on her that autumn.

George Todd was well-known as a very effective trainer, particularly of stayers. He was also clearly a considerable punter. But what was not generally known was that he punted on other people's horses as well as on his own and so often gave back what he had won on his own. He was inordinately fond of his own old horses and instead of retiring them at five, he would get them right for one race or so each year until they were much older. He knew exactly when they were ready to go.

George would often aim them at selling plates or selling hurdles or apprentice or amateur riders' races. One such race took place at Salisbury in the spring. I had no ride but as things seemed quiet in the War Office that morning I took the train down to Salisbury and sat in the weighing room. After a bit, John Hislop, then the leading amateur, came up and asked if I had a ride. When I said "No," he said "George Todd is looking for a jockey. He was not going to run Smithereens until it rained last night. He asked me and I am booked up already. I'll go and find him."

There were at that time no twenty-four hour declarations.

Johnny Hislop, of course, was riding the favourite, Bambi owned by Dorothy Paget. He came back in due course with George Todd and it was agreed that I should ride Smithereens.

"He'll win, you know," George said.

18

In the paddock he just said to me "This horse knows more about it than you do. Let him run his own race just behind the leaders and then come out and win a furlong out: Don't hit him."

George had presumably given Smithereens the same orders, as the old horse settled down just behind the leading four, going away from the stands and round the long bend, at the bottom end of the course. When I saw the tapes of the 1½ mile start, a quarter of a mile from home, I thought it was time to go and pulled out. But very little happened. In desperation I pulled out the whip, and, without falling off, gave him one, put it down and set off for the line. Smithereens, having got the message, put his head down and flew, getting up to beat the odds-on favourite Bambi by something like a length.

When I got back to the unsaddling enclosure, George Todd was there, laughing his head off. Before I got off he said "I told you not to hit him."

"It was the only way I could make him go."

Still laughing, he said, "I don't like my horses hit."

"I am sorry but what's so funny about it?"

"Well, when you went out of the paddock, I saw that in the hurry this morning, we had left Smithereens' heavy shoes on. So instead of having £50 on you, I had £100 on Johnny on the favourite!"

But he forgave me and afterwards in the New Year he asked me to ride an old horse called Queensland in a selling hurdle at Cheltenham — a selling hurdle with £400 added. I said that I would love to ride and turned up at Cheltenham with one or two more winners to go before "losing the five pounds' allowance." I weighed out at the weight on the card less five pounds. But the Clerk of the Scales would not have it. "No," he said, "you will have to draw the full weight because of the value of the race." Who would have thought nowadays that a prize of £400 disqualified the claimer!

George Todd was furious. He said I would have to stand down. But the Clerk of the Scales said that George would have to go to the stewards, as I had technically weighed out and they might not give him permission to change his riding arrangements. The mistake, the Clerk of the Scales said, was his. So George stormed off.

He only reappeared in the paddock just before the jockeys were mounted. All he said was "The old horse knows his way. Let him run his own race. Don't go on too early but don't leave him too much to do up the hill. Let him see the first two, as he has not run for a bit."

At the start I found myself awarded a place on the rails. In the race no-one crossed me, crowded me or bumped me and when Queensland jumped the second hurdle a bit slowly, there was someone upsides at the next to encourage him to jump. Between the last two a gap opened up on the rails and a voice well-known to me said "Go on, sir, go for your life." I did and despite a mistake at the last, won comfortably. George said he had halved his bet because I could not claim, I reckoned that he had other expenses!

A friend of mine from Oxford and army days, Geoff Ford North, a wartime 10th Hussar, used to have a few horses which he trained and rode himself. He was also a keen gambler on the turf and at the tables. One day near the end of 1949 he came up and asked me if I would ride an old horse of his called Petrograd at Worcester, as he could not do the weight. I said I would but then he said you must do exactly as I say."If you look up the old horse's form, you will see that if he strikes the front too soon, he clouts a fence and either falls or knocks the stuffing out of himself. So you must not hit the front until the last. He really only just gets the two miles."

I did as he said, met the last a length behind the leader and trotted up on the run in.

Geoff was delighted and asked me to ride him again the next week at Windsor. I had to tell him that I had now "lost the five" and so he said "All right, I will ride him myself."

It so happened that I was asked to ride an old horse called Kruge in the same race. He was trained by Judy Forwood who had a stable of horses at Stanford in the Pytchley country. The licence was held by Delaney, her head lad — a legitimate ploy at the time when women were not allowed licences in their own names.

On the day of the race I turned up at 9 o'clock at the War Office to be told that the Chief of the Imperial General Staff wanted a brief by 4 o'clock. Luckily it was on a subject which I knew by heart, so I drafted the brief, told my G.S.O. III to put it together and went off to Windsor. In the race Petrograd was one of the best backed and I was the outsider of five at 20-1. Judy said that whatever happened I was to hold him together, in the hope that his legs would stand. He gave me a lovely ride until the second last, which he hit hard but by the time I had collected myself, there was only one in front of me, Petrograd. Knowing that that was just what Geoff did not want, I stayed a length behind until the last, where Petrograd made a real blunder and I went by him to win easily. I returned to a silent War Office room in time for the C.I.G.S. brief. All non-racing people tl 'nk you know when you are going to win, particularly at 20-1!

Kruger did me well that year winning another five races, four of them ridden by me. He also slipped up on the turn at Wolverhampton, breaking my collar-bone and some ribs, so that I missed one winning ride on him. The key to the old horse was that he hung to the left and on a left handed course, you had to stick to the rails — and so look like a jockey! When winning at Wolverhampton, I could not pull out at the last and had to wait until the flat, where luckily, there was a gap on the rails.

I rode Kruger at Liverpool in the Topham. But he frightened himself over The Chair where he made one of the great leaps of all time. After that he started jumping more and more stickily until some loose horse hit us sideways and put us out of the race at Bechers. As a result I was "jocked off" Tommy Traddles which I was due to ride in the National two days later. My substitute belted off from the start and fell at the first. This was no consolation although I did get the ride back at Towcester on Tommy Traddles where he gave me a beautiful ride. As he was about 16.3 hh I

21

always thought he would have been a good ride at Aintree.

Not all days were as good as those at Worcester and at Windsor. I will just mention the two worst.

On Easter Monday I had been offered two rides at Wincanton by a trainer called Wells for whom I had won a race at Newton Abbot. He asked me a long way ahead and so I had to refuse to ride an old horse called Consort at Manchester and another of the same type, Southborough at Plumpton. Needless to say, John Straker won on Consort and the sailor, Dickie Courage, on Southborough.

Meanwhile at Wincanton I was well beaten on Mr. Wells's two and had a fall as well. That was, you may say, par for the course! However I was also asked by what seemed to be a farmer to ride his horse in the selling hurdle. He said it always got round but took a bit of a hold. When my name went up on the numbers board, several jockeys came along and said "What are you riding that for? You won't get to the post, far less get round. It is mad."

It was too late to get off it at that stage. There was nothing for it, I had to go. I saw what they meant on the way to the post and only managed to pull up by cannoning into another horse's quarters.

In the race he took off in front straight away and jumped the first two well. But coming into the straight I found myself with nothing on either side and a space on each side of the hurdle. So I steered for the centre. As we got to the hurdle, he swung left crashing through the wing and the rails into the car park, pursuing a corkscrew course between the cars. I eventually pulled his head against a hut and came to a halt. I jumped off and led him back.

In the weighing-room I was taken aside by the senior steward, the then Lord Digby.

"Did you do that on purpose?"

When I looked amazed he said, "You know you took the favourite and second favourite out with you." I said that I had no idea that I had taken anyone out and that I had been foolish to take a spare ride. So, he went away, shaking his head. I thought afterwards that I should have gone along the rails demanding a case of whisky from each of the principal layers!

After winning on Queensland at Cheltenham, I became very ill and was out of action from Christmas to Easter, which effectively prevented me from becoming a serious amateur. Oddly enough the first day I returned to action at Southwell I had five rides. It would have been six if Cliff Beechener had been able to get hold of me to ride in the last. When I appeared in the weighing-room and said to Arthur Lord who was my valet for the day that I had five rides and needed a light saddle in the third, he thought I was joking.

Sadly it was a day of disaster. The first one, trained by Fiddler Goodwill was trotting up when it broke down coming to the last, the next three just about got round. In the N.H. (Amateurs) flat race, I was riding the second favourite Yedo III trained by Fred Rimell. Atty Corbett was on the odds-on favourite Freddy Fox. Fred told me to try and "slip them" at the last bend. This I tried to do but instead of going as hard as I could as soon as I was round the turn, I increased my speed gradually. I led until the last stride when Atty got up and beat me a head. Fred Rimell was not best pleased!

I stayed for the last and saw Cliff Beechener's animal going well in second place at the second last when his rider gave him a kick and he fell. No doubt, I would have sat still as a stone, "fiddled" the last two and won!

I had ridden one winner for "Fiddler" Goodwill. One day he said he had a good thing at Worcester in an amateurs' hurdle and he hoped I would ride it. I accepted and he was right. I came to the last upsides with Atty, for once going the better, and won easily.

After the race — I hope Fiddler will not mind me telling this story — I was standing on the steps of the weighing room, with the stipendiary steward on one side and all the other stewards on the other when Fiddler came up.

"Thank you very much Colonel," he said, "I won a thousand pounds. You had better have some of it." With that he proceeded to pull out a wad of notes. No-one has ever turned so quickly as I did and bolted into the weighing-room, leaving the notes flying in the air. I just had time to see over my shoulder Fiddler and the stewards scrambling on their knees to gather the fivers. I hope Fiddler got them all back.

I would have been going back to the weighing-room to reward my valet. Jockeys' valets in those days were a remarkable breed and Charlie Stalker was one of the best. He was a wonderfully kind old man, taking as much trouble with an amateur as with the champion jockey. He would lend me a light saddle when necessary, produce my breeches clean after they had been returned covered in mud and blood, arrange for my saddle and tack to go where I was riding, whether he was there or not and, if you had a fall, however busy he was he would come along to the ambulance room with that certain cure for all ills — a cup of tea. When we had all gone home, Charlie and his son David would be busy into the late evening cleaning tack and packing up ready for the next day's work.

At that time, rules or not, there were a few professional amateurs. One in particular would only get up if he was given an encouragement of £50 before the race and a present afterwards. All the same, the current rules now hardly seem to make things better. In those days, to put up an amateur only cost the N.A. insurance money. Now there is no difference in fee for the owner. But forty years of Socialism have altered the facts of life, so that there are few owner riders such as Anthony Mildmay and few soldier-riders. On the other hand a man who is paid as an assistant trainer can ride as an amateur, though he is limited in the number of open races in which he can ride. The rules are, quite rightly, drawn in favour of the professional. But is is sad to see the amateur element confined to hunter chasers and the Grand Military. Let us have a few more owner riders.

I did not have as many rides in hunter chases as I should have liked. Epsom is not the best centre for hunting. But one day I was rung up by Major Harold Rushton to ask me to ride his very good horse Monks Crest at Leicester in 1950. Atty Corbett, who usually had the ride, had hurt himself. Harold Rushton had owned, trained and had ridden a long string of hunter chasers and point-to-pointers, including such as Odell who won the Foxhunters at Aintree in 1937 & '38. Harold Rushton had hunted and shot with my father-in-law, Iney Palethorpe, himself a great point-to-point rider of earlier days in Worcestershire and I am sure that Harold Rushton had only asked me because of this connection. I had a good ride on Monk's Crest and won but Atty got the ride back — it was his ride — and won several times more, including at the National Hunt Festival of 1950.

Two months later Atty was due to ride him at Manchester on the Saturday of the Bank Holiday Meeting in early April. I went to Southwell and won on Kruger. Later that evening while we were celebrating, the telephone rang. It was Harold Rushton. I said "How did Monk's Crest get on?"

"That is why I am after you. Atty fell off him halfway round."

"I am sure he did not fall off."

"Oh yes he did. But the old horse had not done a turn and if you can ride him at Chepstow on Monday in the hunter chase, I will run him there."

I got off my Monday rides at Hereford and went to Chepstow where the old horse carried me round to victory in the Chepstow Hunters' Chase for the Tredegar Cup. He was almost too tired to jump the last but he was truly game.

At the beginning of another hunter chasing season, Rushton asked me to ride him at Newbury. He said "It is only two and a half miles, too short for him, and he will need the race, but do your best. I am also interested in a young horse ridden by a chap who has just come over from Ireland."

On the way to the post I was surprised to see that we were favourite. He gave me a lovely ride and between the last two seemed to have a chance. Then, as forecast he "blew up." As he was stopping his other horse came past me at a million miles an hour. It trotted up.

Harold Rushton did not come to see me unsaddle the old horse. But when he did appear I asked him if he had "a nice touch".

25

"Yes," he said "very satisfactory". Which goes to show that all hunting majors are not fools.

As I have mentioned Anthony Mildmay two or three times, I would not like to give the impression that he was anything but a marvellous example of the true amateur, the best thing imaginable for National Hunt racing. But, like Harold Rushton, he was no fool. One strong prejudice he had was against flat racing which he referred to as "flapping". No doubt he always wore a black tie on the first day of the flat racing season. One day he was riding in an amateurs' hurdle at Sandown, in which Teddy Underdown was to ride the favourite, trained by Walter Nightingall. Now Teddy had some valuable film contracts at the time and they precluded him from riding jumping though he rode a good many winners on the flat. Anthony, therefore, considered him as part of "flapping". I rode an animal for Tom Hanbury which belonged to an American.

Tom, father of the trainer of the 1986 Oaks winner Midway Lady, said, "He has no chance but the owner likes to see his colours in front. So jump off and go as far as you can in front."

So, off I went and between the last two hurdles was still in the lead, when I heard a tremendous rumpus behind me. Anthony was shouting "Don't let the flapping b . . . . . out! Keep him where he is!" But Teddy had a stone in hand, found his way out and won easily. I was third.

Perhaps it would be appropriate to conclude my account of voyages round the gaffes by relating a story concerned with the flat. I was instructing at the Staff College when the Commandant told me that I had been selected to give the Infantry Battalion lecture at the Royal Naval Staff College at Greenwich. I looked up the date and found it coincided with the date of an amateur's race at Lewes. Rather cheekily I wrote and asked if I could perform in the morning rather than the afternoon. The Admiral replied charmingly, saying that he looked forward to seeing me for lunch in the famous "Painted Hall." In his introductory remarks he mentioned that he was sorry that I had to return to the Staff College "to lecture" immediately after lunch.

In the Navy it is customary to divide time for lectures into two parts, one for the talker and the other half for questions, so that directing staff can find out who slept throughout the talk. After my three quarters of an hour, I nervously awaited questions. The first man to get up seemed to have a familiar face and looking at the "crib" in front of me showing who was who, I realised that it was H.R.H. Prince Philip, who was on the course. He was fairly short and easy to answer, so that he was able to return his thoughts to more important things for the rest of the period. The next one was an easy one. But the third came from someone at the back.

"What chance," he said, "have you got at Lewes this afternoon?"

The horse I was riding was a well-known handicapper called Fast Soap, trained by Gordon Johnson Houghton. He needed a race before tackling something bigger and Gordon thought, very kindly, he would give me a chance of riding a winner. The only snag was that according to the conditions he had to carry 13 stones 3 lbs! a fact of which I was fully aware when it came to carrying the saddle back to weigh in.

In the race all went well until the last hundred yards when something ridden by Teddy Underdown in receipt of a great deal of weight came striding past to beat me.

Gordon was very good about it. Nonetheless, I was to say the least, very disappointed and sat in the weighing room, looking at my hands. All Hastings are known to have small hands and feet, resulting from generations of avoidance of manual labout — I have not noticed if my Bass relations have hands like brewers! At that moment I was handed a telegram. Would it be from the Admiral, who had lost his money or the Staff College ordering my immediate return? When I opened it, all it said was "Larger hands for faster soap!"

I have referred to Fiddler Goodwill earlier on. He did, however, do me what turned out to be a very good turn on a November day in 1948, one that has stood me well for 38

27

years. I was changing somewhere when Fiddler came into the changing room and approached Anthony Mildmay.

"My Lord," he said, "I have a horse running at Doncaster which I would like you to ride. He will win."

Anthony said "What's the horse? What weight has it got?"

"It is called Eight Reigns and has 10 stone 13lbs in a three mile amateur hurdle. It will win, you know."

"I can't get near that weight — try him." He pointed across the room at me.

I did not know Fiddler then and saw him ask who I was and then come over to me.

"Do you want to ride a winner, Colonel?" he enquired. Naturally I did.

It was a good three weeks before the race on a Saturday at Doncaster. The day before I was due to ride something with no chance at Sandown. As I was standing, dressed to ride in the members enclosure, Lady Margaret Fortescue came up with someone whom I had seen and admired before but whom I had never met. They had had a bad day and were "touting". I told them I had no chance at all. So they asked if I knew anything at Sandown that day or the next. I did not and was just about to be dismissed as a boring soldier with no information when I said "I am not coming here tomorrow. I am going to Doncaster."

"What could bring you there?"

"I am riding something in the stayers' hurdle — the second race. The trainer seems to think it will win."

Margaret looked at me as if I could not be riding a trier, let alone a winner, but the other girl asked its name.

"Eight Reigns" I said and departed quickly.

On the Saturday there was a thick fog and my train was desperately late. They had only just started jumping at Doncaster and I did not know the course nor was there time to walk it. I was, therefore, somewhat stumped when Fiddler said "Hold him up. Don't hit the front until after the last or he will stop. But don't worry, he will win."

Three miles hurdles are to my mind somewhat boring to

watch or to ride in and this one in a thick fog seemed to go on for ever. I settled down just behind the leaders, but slopping along in the mud and the fog I had no idea when the last hurdle would be reached. You could not see the stands but you could hear the crowd when we emerged from the gloom. At last I saw some of the other amateurs go for their whips and so gave him a kick into what proved to be the last hurdle. He responded well and we won by a neck, a neck and a neck. The owner, who was the proprietor of a pub in Doncaster, came out to lead me in. For him it could have been like winning the St. Leger. Fiddler had had a good bet.

Meanwhile at Sandown all were assembled ready for the off. But the fog did not lift. In despair, just as the abandonment was announced, my two girl friends of the day before went over to the books and inquired about the price of Eight Reigns at Doncaster. One of them had a nice bet at 8-1 and clearly, from that moment, decided to take me on for good. Her name was Jean.

CHAPTER 3

The British Bloodstock Agency

THE ARMY had been kind to me since the War and had let me off lightly with home postings, Staff College, War Office and the Green Jackets Depot at Winchester. I knew therefore that on my next posting I would be sent abroad in a minor capacity. I imagined myself three years in Germany counting socks or alternatively two years on the Suez Canal counting oil cans! There was a further and more serious problem; Jean and I had by now acquired a King Charles spaniel, Rupert, and I knew that my wife would never part with him to go into quarantine. If the choice was between myself and Rupert I knew who would win, so when I had an offer of a job I considered it carefully.

While at the Green Jackets Depot I had rented a house near Winchester from the Craig-Harvey family, one of whom was working for the British Bloodstock Agency, a firm of which I had hardly heard. Hugh Craig-Harvey also much enjoyed riding his own steeplechasers, the best known of whom rejoiced in the name of Lord Turbot. I had turned down two offers from Merchant Banks, as I did not somehow fancy office life and huge luncheons. This time I asked both my cousin, Peter Hastings-Bass, then training at Kingsclere and my accountant what they thought of the BBA. Peter gave me mild encouragement but the accountant turned it down flat as "too much of a risk business."

With Rupert in mind, I took the job. The pay was £2,500 a year, some car expenses and some racecourse entrances paid. It was not a prospect of great prosperity.

The BBA had been going since 1911 when I joined it. A journalist called E.E. Coussell had started it. He had little knowledge of horses but could quote pedigrees for several generations back and liked rolling them off his tongue. He also founded the Bloodstock Breeders' Review. Despite the Great War, the BBA managed to survive and, with a partner called Crawford, carried on the BBA business between the wars.

When I joined the partners they were somewhat elderly gentlemen; Brigadier Scott, Gerald McElligott and Colonel "Angie" Lloyd.

Brigadier "Scottie" Scott had been born in the 19th century in the North of England and joined a Lowland regiment. In India the doctors found that he had a weak chest and could not serve in a combat unit. He was offered several alternatives in the Indian Civil Service and other government services but chose to join the Remounts. He served with them throughout two wars and ended up as Director of Remounts in the Indian Army, decorated with the C.I.E. In his Indian career he gained more knowledge of horses and mules than most people. He had a detailed veterinary knowledge and knew all about practical feeding and maintenance. He travelled to Australia, to the USA and to Argentina in search of horses and mules. In between a busy life of race-riding, hunting, polo and shooting, his main job for many years was selecting remounts from the various sources open to him in India, Australia, the USA and the Argentine.

One story he told was of selecting horses for the Army from Indian breds. He would see these unbroken, un-named and unmarked young horses and select those which came within the specifications. When he had seen one lot in a village, he would then be asked into the headman's house or tent. There a long discussion would ensue over which he should take and at what price. He always thought this unnecessary as the price range was determined by the Government beforehand. After a bit he discovered that while he was being put on the spot by the headman, some of those which he had not selected were driven to the next village and mingled with the horses to be inspected there.

If he had passed one at the second village of those which he had turned down at the first, he would have lost his name all

31

over India. So, when years afterwards, he was asked to describe a horse, he always began by giving its markings.

His particular gift was in selecting stallions and mares, not only for export but for import. He picked out Prince Chevalier and Donatello II.

When asked by the great Italian breeder, Signor Tesio, for whom he had often dealt, if his horse Nearco had a place outside Italy, Scottie wisely recommended that he should be raced outside Italy to test his class. The race chosen rather surprisingly was the Grand Prix de Paris of 1938 over one mile seven furlongs. Scottie persuaded the leading book-maker of his day, Martin Benson, to try to buy the horse if he impressed in the Grand Prix. His offer was to be £50,000, but only if Scottie approved his conformation and his racecourse performance. When Nearco won easily, Signor Tesio put up the price to £60,000. Scottie got on the telephone from the racecourse to Mr. Benson in England, no mean achievement in itself, and explained the situation. Mr. Benson was unwilling to raise his offer, until Scottie suggested that he would guarantee to sell ten shares in the horse, if Mr. Benson went ahead. So he did so — with remarkable results for Europe and racing.

Scottie was very small with a piercing expression, always neat and collected in any crisis. He was unfortunately deaf but heard almost anything he wanted to hear. His type of horse tended to be one with an Arab head, straight hocks and short cannons, he went first for "quality" and thought the ideal height for a broodmare was 15.2 hands.

Despite being despaired of by the Indian Army, Scottie lived until ninety, no doubt largely because he could go away on BBA business after the December Sales and thus miss the worst of the weather.

Gerald McElligott was another partner. He also had Indian experience in the Veterinary Corps of the Indian Army. He was very much an Irishman and entirely different in outlook to Scottie. He was a brilliant judge of a horse, sometimes accepting faults which would have turned away others. He would take a fancy to a horse and say "that would win a Cup. " It usually did. He would often buy something of which Scottie's more orthodox eye disapproved. When asked what was the most important thing to look for in a horse, he said "symmetry, " meaning that it should be well-balanced.

A great deal of Gerald's time was occupied by his work as manager for Mr. Robert Sterling Clark, a member of the family who first introduced sewing machines to the world. When I joined the BBA he was an old man and lived in America. He had bred Anglo-Arabs and when the New York Jockey Club would not accept them for the Stud Book, he abandoned racing in America and turned to England, Ireland and France.

When the war came he had to return his mares to America and by the time I joined the firm, he kept most of his breeding stock at the Graysons' stud near Upperville in Virginia. They came over to England and Ireland as yearlings to be trained. He had three trainers, Michael Collins in Ireland (whom he always referred to as St Michael), Harry Peacock in Yorkshire and Joe Lawson, who had by now moved from Manton to Newmarket. The young stock would come over to the BBA's farm at Enfield, where the trainers would make their choice, taking it in rotation annually as to who should have first pick.

In 1952 when the yearlings came over and concentrated at our Glasgow Paddocks stud at Enfield in Middlesex, Michael Collins and Joe Lawson came to choose but Harry Peacock asked if Gerald McElligott would choose for him, as he did not want to leave England (i.e. Yorkshire!) When they were led round Gerald, acting for Harry Peacock, had the first choice and picked out a dark chestnut with a little white about him, not very tall and almost "back at the knee. " He was by Nasrullah.

When he rang up Harry to tell him which he was getting, the old man let out a roar. "I don't want a Nasrullah "he said, "the last one I had was mad. " So Gerald exchanged his original choice for the next one and sent the Nasrullah colt to

Joe Lawson. That is why Never Say Die was trained in Newmarket and not in Yorkshire.

Gerald "managed" all the Clark horses and kept a close eye on Never Say Die, who started off both at two and in his early three-year-old days on a fairly low note. Early in May, he started to improve and before he ran in the Newmarket Stakes, Joe Lawson said he thought him a classic colt — about 33-1 at that! His subsequent racecourse career is well-known. He won the Derby on merit, ridden by the then eighteen year old Lester Piggott, but after his unfortunate defeat at Royal Ascot, which resulted in Lester Piggott being "stood down" there did not seem to Lawson a suitable race in which his stamina could be tested in public. He was therefore sent to Yarmouth Racecourse where the stand-in jockey Charlie Smirke was to ride him in a gallop of 1¾ miles. The top class handicapper Lepidoptic — afterwards a stallion in Australia — was to jump in for the last mile. Charlie Smirke jumped on and set off down the course. Being Smirke he did not ask where to start but went down to what was, in fact, the 2 mile gate! He came back in bounding form having trounced Lepidoptic over the last mile. So we knew he would stay 1¾ in the St Leger. Lepidoptic went on to win the Great Yorkshire Handicap over the St Leger course off top-weight easily. We were therefore confident that Never Say Die would win Robert Sterling Clark his second classic, as indeed he did, winning the St Leger by no less than twelve lengths from the runner-up Elopement.

After the St Leger there were several further opportunities for Never Say Die. But Mr. Clark refused to run him. The Queen was leading owner at that stage of the season and if Never Say Die had won a valuable race, he would have put Mr. Clark above her on the list. Mr. Clark was determined that this should not happen. Furthermore, he did not agree to the horse staying in training at four years of age, though he appeared to be only just coming to himself by the St Leger.

Mr. Clark wanted to see his first foals, and being an old

man, knew that there was no time to waste. He therefore insisted on retiring his horse from training at the end of his three-year-old career and giving him to the English National Stud, only keeping for himself the right to a few nominations for himself and his friends. He did not forget his Irish friends and made it a condition of his gift that seven nominations were reserved annually for Irish breeders. Few more generous gestures have ever been made in the history of English thoroughbred breeding.

Apart from his successes as Mr. Clark's manager, Gerald McElligott bought both Nasrullah and Royal Charger for Irish studs, who sold them on to the USA. When he was already a cripple from arthritis he went over to see Nasrullah and hobbled on his two sticks to his box. He could not attract the attention of anyone and so walked into his box. Normally Nasrullah would go for anyone who did such a thing and probably savage him. The horrified stud manager came rushing over when he heard someone in the stallion box only to find Gerald poking the horse in the ribs to make him stand up properly!

Gerald was not such a good judge of women as he was of horses and caused himself endless trouble throughout his life. Nor was he ever a competent driver. He seemed to think that the road was a competition and as a result never went as much as two months without landing in the ditch or turning over the car. Once when Hugh Craig-Harvey was driving they were approaching a level crossing, when the gates began to close.

"Go for your life," roared Gerald.

And so Craig-Harvey did, just scraping through before they shut!

The third partner was Colonel "Angie" Lloyd, so named because he sang treble at school. He had been a regular soldier, a Horse Gunner and on retirement had looked after various stud farms. So he knew the language and the people. Scottie brought him in to try to bring some order and organization into the affairs of the BBA. He did not travel but ran the office. Under the guise of a typical regular soldier, a "blow-hole Charlie," he hid an extremely shrewd brain with a knowledge of mathematics not shared by Gerald McElligott. To hear him talking on the telephone when buying or selling was to listen to a great dealer at his best. He always knew what he wanted, either to buy at a lower price than that on offer or to persuade a buyer to give just a little more than he had said he would. He was also an adept at dealing with the Bank and with Tattersalls, not to mention the clients after a huge December Sales.

There was also Hugh Craig-Harvey, who was soon to retire to the country to run his own stud in the West country, Rackenford Manor. I am glad to say he is still a client of the BBA.

Another partner was George Blackwell, who had been brought in to edit the BBA annual, *The Bloodstock Breeders Review*. His vast knowledge of pedigrees enabled him to do a very good job at this or rather would have, if he had not let the annual get further and further behind, while prefering to sell bloodstock. The sight of yet another military figure joining the firm was too much for George and shortly after I arrived, he left.

When he gave up his job with the BBA I was sent immediately to Australia, and to New Zealand to reassure the clients that we were still active. Some aspects of Australian racing are described later in this book. In the meantime, I was introduced to Humphrey Finney, the President of Fasig Tipton, the American bloodstock auctioneer. When he came over for the December Sales, he also met my wife and being possessed of a remarkable cunning and knowledge of American psychology he said to Scottie "You should send the two over to America to stay for the Maryland Hunt Cup and the Kentucky Derby. I will introduce them and show them round."

The old gentlemen were horrified at the idea of a partner travelling with his wife. After all they set off each year to avoid their wives or in Gerald's case mistresses! And the expense! But Humphrey persuaded them and much against their will, we set off to the United States to sail to New

York. We travelled cabin class, a grave mistake. You met no prospective clients down there and when we arrived at the docks, the reception party was waiting at the First class exit.

Humphrey Finney immediately took us in hand. The Board of Fasig Tipton were having a meeting in New York and I was introduced to the members, but we did also have a few introductions of our own.

After a few days we went down to Maryland to see the Hunt Cup and learned for the first time the facts of American life, previously unknown to us. The remarkable hospitality and kindness shown by Americans — at least East Coast Americans — is in distinct contradiction to the way in which many Englishmen freeze at the presence of a foreigner. All sorts of people would go out of their way to help us, driving many miles to do so, having us to stay and giving parties for us.

What I had also not appreciated was the difference in drinking habits between us and them. For one thing, their alcoholic drinks were, and still are, very much stronger than ours, they were dowsed liberally with ice, and were normally put down before meals and not afterwards. The habit of drinking wine had not by then come into fashion.

The third feature was that nearly all policemen were of Irish origin and the best chance of getting away with a motoring offence was to produce an Irish driving licence!

Maryland is a beautiful state, notable for its wild dogwood, and the Maryland Hunt Cup takes place in an attractive setting for spectators, who are apt to arrive from long distances armed with Bourbon whisky and mint. For the riders it is less attractive, since all the fences are stiff, constructed of more or less unbreakable timber. There is only one race but the spectators manage to make it a day's entertainment. The race has shown that it is a proving ground for National horses and jockeys, including such as Billy Barton, runner up to Tipperary Tim in the 1928 Grand National, and Ben Nevis, winner in 1980.

From Maryland, we went south to stay at various places in Virginia. Among our hosts were Danny and Peggy Van Clief who lived not far from Charlottesville in Virginia. They had a stud farm and consigned yearlings annually to Saratoga Sales, held by the Fasig Tipton Company of which Danny was a director. They were extremely kind to us, both in Virginia and at Saratoga. Now Danny's eldest son Daniel G. Van Clief II is well-known as the co-ordinator of the Breeders Cup and another son runs the stud.

While staying with them, they discussed coming to England for the hottest months in Virginia which coincided with our most important racing season. For several years they came over, twice taking Tichborne Park near us in Hampshire from the Tichbornes and at other times an old house in Winchester. This naturally led them to take an interest in racing a few horses in England. I had therefore to find a suitable trainer. I advised them to go to Geoffrey Brooke, whom they knew and liked already. He was at Clarehaven, Newmarket, by then with a full stable of horses mainly just below top-class but with probably the nicest collection of owners you could find anywhere. Major Dermot McCalmont trained there as did various Anglo Irish and Irish owners. A cocktail party for Geoffrey's owners would have been fun to attend.

Geoffrey had for many years been assistant to his brother-in-law Atty Persse, a past master at preparing a two-year-old to win first time out. Geoffrey then trained for the Yorkshire owner breeder Major L.B. Holliday for a year or two, turning out for him the 1951 Oaks winner Neasham Belle. After setting up on his own, he won the 1955 Two Thousand Guineas for Sir David Robinson with Our Babu.

Geoffrey had rather a forbidding appearance which masked a great sense of humour and a very well organised Winchester-educated brain. He managed to maintain the appearance of relaxed calm at the most critical moments in Newmarket life. Once he was having his after-luncheon sleep, of which he was very fond, when his new assistant rushed in and said " Geoffrey, two yearlings have arrived and all the boxes are full. Where shall we put them?"

"Turn them loose in the High Street" said Geoffrey and

38

went back to sleep, knowing the man could not help but find somewhere for them in Newmarket.

On another occasion, Geoffrey had two runners in a race at Newmarket, one nearly favourite ridden by Doug Smith and one with no apparent chance ridden by Paddy Newson. Geoffrey noticed that some "spiv" with no right in the paddock was standing very close to the parade ring listening to their conversation. So he said loudly to Paddy Newson, "Now, ride a nice race on him. Don't make much use of him early on and come out and win in the last two furlongs." Paddy could not believe his ears — even less when Geoffrey turned to Doug and said "You know what to do, strangle the bugger."

No spiv has ever run so fast from the paddock to the books as Geoffrey's eavesdropper. But in the race, Doug won and Paddy was in the last three.

One of the most difficult tasks for an agent is to fit the owner to the trainer. In most cases, the owner comes to the agent, probably from abroad and asks him to buy a horse or two and find a trainer. The agent has to choose someone who will get on with the owner, do a good job with the horses and will not steal the business from the agent when his back is turned. Most foreign owners are inclined to be a burden to the trainer and his telephone account by inquiring as to the progress of his horses at odd and inconvenient moments according to the time in his own country. Geoffrey Brooke said that to have a manager or an agent looking after an owner's horses was to some extent an advantage. He could always be made to break the news to the owner when the horse had been beaten a short head or broken his leg on the gallops.

My choice of Geoffrey for Danny Van Clief was a great success in this case. No-one could have got on better than Geoffrey and Danny did. What is more he did very well for him on the racecourse. Most of his horses were bought at auction as yearlings or homebred and unsuitable for racing in America.

Among the best horses we bought for Danny was a colt by

High Treason out of Belle Noisette, one of a series which took a bit of naming. Danny and Peggy would often come up with a good name straight away, but when this, as almost always happened, was turned down by Weatherbys, they would be inclined to forget and leave it to me to name it. In this case as it was the time when certain smooth men in the Foreign Office were defecting to Russia and Belle Noisette seemed to have some connection with the ballet, I tried Light On His Feet, little knowing that such an expression in America was used to indicate a homosexual. Danny was initially pretty cross at having to read Mr. D.G. Van Clief's Light On His Feet. But he soon got used to the idea and I told him that anyone who knew him by sight would not believe it!

Danny and Peggy came over to Tichborne when Light On His Feet was a two-year-old, in 1961 complete with their own aeroplane and coloured servants including Ben and Lorraine Paige, his driver and maid, both of them great successes in rural Hampshire. The day after arrival we all set off for Manchester races where Light On His Feet was due to run in the Whitsuntide Stakes, a valuable race at that time. The weather was bad and we were routed right round London before turning north. Peggy was never very happy out of sight of land and when we were over Birmingham in thick cloud she requested that we land immediately. The pilot could not get permission for our immediate landing without giving a compelling reason, so he said with great tact that it would be quicker to go on to Manchester where we landed in time to see Light On His Feet in the paddock. Danny, whose first sight of the horse this was, was not greatly impressed, but happy with the outcome as he won easily. Later he won another good race for him at Newmarket but did no good at all when sent to America.

Danny and I were at the sales one day in 1961 when a chestnut colt with a light-coloured mane and tail came into the ring. We had liked him beforehand and Geoffrey knew a lot about him because he was bred by his wife's nephew Lord Harrington. As he walked round, Danny, always mindful that he "might be 'had' by those 'God damn'

40

English — though they are no worse than the Irish", was doubtful about his limit. He decided we would go to 3,000 guineas. At 2,800, it was our bid and the auctioneer seemed just about to knock him down, when he suddenly said:-
"3,000. I am bid 3,000."
Whether he had taken the bid from a genuine buyer or from a friend of the owners or even by acknowledging the gesture of someone wiping a fly from his nose, I do not know. Anyway, Danny let forth a flow of good Virginian language, saying "We nearly had him." I thought very quickly that we could not leave it at that and put in another bid.
"Whose bid is that?" said Danny.
"Yours," I said.
While we were arguing about the rights and wrongs of my going beyond his limit, the horse was knocked down to the BBA. I, of course, offered to pay the difference but Danny saw the light and kept all the horse. He was named Crocket and became one of the most remarkable two-year-olds of the era. Starting at York in the Knavesmire Stakes, he won very easily, then went on to the Coventry at Royal Ascot, where he was equally impressive. He had a long rest then before his next main objective, the Gimcrack, but began to work lazily at home, so that another small race was found for him to win at Yarmouth. He won the Gimcrack and the Middle Park, neither of them in a style that pleased the press, but retired for the season, the unbeaten winner of five races, four of them good class. Oddly enough Geoffrey believed that a good two-year-old should not run more than four or five times in his first season.
Crocket began the next season by winning at Newmarket. It was not a very impressive performance but he still remained favourite for the 2000 Guineas, now the winner of six consecutive races.
The Van Cliefs came over in force for the Guineas. The only thing Geoffrey Brooke was worried about was heavy going — and so, of course, the rain came down in buckets all that night and all the next morning. Crocket was a very short priced favourite, went down well to the post but in the race

dropped out to be last. Surprisingly neither stewards' enquiry nor dope test took place. No apparent explanation existed for his performance.

When Crocket trailed in last in the 2000 Guineas, Geoffrey was accosted by one of those ladies who infest the "members" of many racecourses.

"Geoffrey. What a terrible thing! What happened?"

"I do not know, Madam, but if you can't be first there is some distinction in being last!"

The next month at Royal Ascot Crocket ran in blinkers in the St James's Palace Stakes, was jumped off in front and beat a good field by six lengths. He ran once more at Goodwood and put up a similar performance to that in the Guineas. This time there was a dope test but it showed no positive result. Of course rumours circulated that he was "got at" in the 2000 Guineas. There was no positive evidence either way. Most of his progeny were genuine on the racecourse but breeders remembered his Guineas performance, so that he did not have the mares he deserved when he stood at stud in Limerick in Ireland. After a few years there the Japanese, at that time at the height of their European buying effort, bought him to go to stud. He had a useful if not outstanding career in Japan.

Danny had other useful horses including Stoned by Nearctic ex Hawkestone, which he bred himself. Stoned seemed a suitable name, so Stoned he was called. I did not know that Stoned was a well-known American expression for a drunk. Once again Danny took mild exception at the statement on the card that Mr. Van Clief's Stoned but did admit that on occasions he might have been! Stoned was a useful horse and trained by Peter Walwyn won his share of races, including good ones at Ascot and at St. Cloud and was not disgraced in Blakeney's Derby in 1969.

When Geoffrey Brooke retired in 1967, the plan was for Peter Walwyn to take over all the horses. But when Doug Smith decided to train — a last minute decision — Danny kept some with him. As a result, when Mrs. Jackie Ward, as she was then, offered Doug the lease of a filly by Crocket out of the famous old mare Zanzara, called Farfalla, he first offered the chance to me and then to Danny. Farfalla soon proved herself in the spring of 1969 a very good filly on the gallops. One question was when to run her, as she would need a race before the Queen Mary at Ascot. Danny was coming over and the only date when he thought he could be present was that of a race at Alexandra Park in May. At the last minute, Danny could not come and I felt sorry for the owners of the others in the race, who had to meet such a good filly at Ally Pally! She won easily and headed for the Queen Mary. At that time Paddy Newson was riding work for Doug Smith and Peter Walwyn. He sat on both Humble Duty, a BBA buy and subsequently the winner of the 1000 Guineas, and Farfalla. I don't know which he picked before the race but Farfalla won well with Humble Duty third.

After having had several years racing over here and many winners Danny decided in 1970 to sell out completely and concentrate on his stud. I found an owner for the whole lot — Mr. (now Sir David) Wills. One of them, Rotisserie, won the Fred Darling at Newbury the next year and another won four or five races. But it would be hard to say who had the best or worst of the deal.

Before leaving the story of the Van Cliefs, another naming adventure is worth a mention. I bought a yearling by Doutelle out of a well-known old mare called Credit Lyonnais. I thought that D. G. Van Clief's Doubtful Credit would sound a good joke, as the last thing to doubt was his credit. Danny agreed. She turned out to be very moderate but before we found that out she ran in the Queen Mary at Royal Ascot in 1964. Two days later a special messenger turned up at our office bearing a large envelope. Inside was a letter on the following lines :-

"I am the manager of Credit Lyonnais in London. I attended Royal Ascot. I was horrified to see that there was a horse running out of the mare Credit Lyonnais, called Doubtful Credit. " And so on for a page or two.

This was beyond me to answer but Danny wrote a letter of such masterly tact that all was forgiven. Doubtful Credit herself was sold at the end of her three-year-old days and was last seen running in a hurdle race at Folkestone.

CHAPTER 4

American Friends

DANNY AND PEGGY VAN CLIEF were not the only hospitable people I met in Virginia. They included that very remarkable lady, Marion du Pont Scott. One day whilst staying at Nydrie with Danny and Peggy, I was greeted in the morning by the following statement from my host.

"Now Hastings, you have really got to behave today — no dirty stories please, and no getting drunk!"

"Why?"

"Because we are going over to have lunch with Mrs. du Pont Scott at Montpelier and you will need to be on your best behaviour."

I had, of course, heard of this lady as she had sent over Battleship to win the 1937 Grand National, ridden by Bruce Hobbs and trained by his father Reg. Marion du Pont Scott was a great name in American racing, particularly in steeplechasing. She had owned a large number of the best horses running over obstacles as well as some good horses on the flat, including a top class colt in Mongo. I was told that she was a very scrupulous judge of conformation in a horse, her ideal being one who would win in the show ring in the lightweight hunter class. She liked a quality horse with good hocks — rare for an American — and very good forelegs. Perhaps her requirement for a good leg derived from her interest in hunters. She had her own pack of hounds at Montpelier with which you could go out hunting at her invitation only. Her hunt servants were nearly always mounted on her ex-steeplechasers — some with famous names in American chasing such as Annapolis.

Every year there was run in the autumn at Montpelier, the Montpelier Hunt Meet. The races were held in the park and consisted of five races — flat, hurdles and steeplechasing.

There was no entry fee to run a horse and the prize money up to ten or fifteen thousand dollars for the principal race was given by Mrs. Scott. On the day of the race-meeting people came from far and wide and picnicked in the park. They were charged no entrance fee either for cars or passengers. All was paid for by Mrs. Scott. As the races were under the American equivalent of National Hunt rules, bookmakers, as at an English point-to-point meeting, took up their positions.

Anyone who had a runner in the races was invited to lunch at the house and, after the races, a large number of locals were asked to tea. Not to be asked, if you were a local, was the equivalent of being black-balled for Whites, except that it was a more frequent occurrence. Dinner was at 7 or 7.30 pm and the guests sat round a large turkey. After dinner, at exactly 9 o'clock, Mrs. Scott and all her house-party departed to bed, many of them casting longing looks at the sideboard where bottles of bourbon whisky stood unfinished. But I have never known anyone brave enough to ask to stay behind for a night cap.

Marion du Pont Scott had two other residences, one at Saratoga, where she sent her horses in August, and one in South Carolina, where she owned the racecourse where the Colonial Cup is run and the training track, where many large stables wintered their horses. At Saratoga she had a yard and a cottage near the Oklahoma training track. On the wall of the sitting room of the cottage were prints of the Garth Hounds in full cry near where the du Ponts had once lived in Berkshire. In South Carolina she had a large and beautifully furnished house but sadly when I stayed there she was not well enough to come down. Nevertheless I was royally entertained.

Mrs. Scott had married the actor, Randolph Scott, but this arrangement had come to an end many years before I met her. She did not marry again, but she had a friend who lived in a cottage some quarter of a mile away from the big house. He was called Carol Bassett and had in his day been a great amateur steeplechase rider and later a very talented sculptor

45

of animals. By the time I knew him, he was virtually bed-ridden.

Every day at four o'clock, when Marion was in residence, one or two of the maids in uniform with skirts down to their ankles, sallied forth with the accoutrements of a tea-party, put the kettle on and laid out the table. At 4.30, Mrs. Scott came down from the house and there they sat drinking tea and talking of Maryland Hunt Cups and Temple Gwathmey Steeplechases of years ago, whilst her Border terriers played or squabbled under the table.

We were shown round the house full of good European and American colonial furniture, the walls hung with sporting pictures, many of them of fighting cocks. Upstairs was some of the original furniture installed by President Madison when he built the house. Indeed we twice had the honour of sleeping in Madison's bed. The only difficulty here was that it had considerable "sag" in the middle and if either turned over sharply both occupants were liable to slide together towards the middle until they met with a clash!

One day in January 1974 when I was staying at Montpelier, Marion Scott told me that she had in Soothsayer a very good chaser, who, carrying top weight, had just been beaten in the Colonial Cup at Camden the previous November as a seven-year-old. She wanted to send Soothsayer to England to win, not the National, which she had done already, but the Cheltenham Gold Cup. She asked me to recommend a trainer. I suggested Fred Winter and was instructed to ask him if he would take Soothsayer.

Fred agreed, so Soothsayer came to England at the beginning of 1974 and on his first appearance over English fences showed himself to be a class horse by winning the two miles Cathcart Challenge Cup at the National Hunt Meeting at Cheltenham. Ridden by Richard Pitman, then Fred's stable jockey, Soothsayer won from the old Cheltenham Gold Cup winner L'Escargot. It was a great achievement on the part of horse, trainer and jockey.

It had been a day of mixed fortune for the stable for earlier in the afternoon the Fred Winter trained Pendil, an odds-on

46

favourite for the Cheltenham Gold Cup, had been brought down close to home when going like a winner.

The next season in spite of Pendil, Marion du Pont Scott insisted that Soothsayer was entered in the Cheltenham Gold Cup. John Francome was just beginning to make his mark as Fred Winter's up and coming jockey and rode Soothsayer in all his preliminary races before the Gold Cup, having a nasty fall on him at Sandown, being beaten on him narrowly three times but winning a minor race at Wincanton from the Queen Mother's favourite Game Spirit.

As the National Hunt Meeting drew near in 1975 it was clear Fred Winter had three strings to his bow in the Gold Cup: Pendil, who was to be ridden by Pitman; the old champion hurdler Bula, who had taken well to fences under Francome; and Soothsayer, whose form did not look good enough. Then three weeks before Cheltenham Pendil broke down and Pitman became free to ride Soothsayer.

On Gold Cup day on very heavy ground which caused some races to be abandoned, the Gold Cup was thought to rest between the Irish trained pair, Captain Christie and Ten Up, with Bula third favourite and Soothsayer a remote 28-1 outsider in the field of eight. Unfortunately Marion Scott was not able to come over for the meeting, in which Soothsayer ran the race of his life, looked a possible winner two out, made a mistake at the last but still finished a close second to the winner Ten Up with Bula third. Marion Scott's insistence in letting Soothsayer take his chance in the Gold Cup had very nearly had a fairy tale ending, but it was not to be.

Marion Scott, like many American owners, had her own ideas about training and placing her horses and many trainers had her horses for a short time. Downie (Frank) Bonsal, who had ridden winners of the Maryland Hunt Cup, was her longest standing trainer and latterly Peter Howe did the job of trainer and stud manager together.

For years her great friend was Helen Whitaker, owner of that marvellous jumper Tingle Creek who, trained at Newmarket by Tom Jones, excelled at Sandown. Helen

Whitaker lived not too far away from Montpelier in a house where at night you could hear the sound of music of the Coon Hounds running in circles round the woods, while their owners sat round the fire drinking. One day Marion and Helen had a disagreement about when their horses were to run, as a result of which Mrs. Whitaker's horse beat Mrs. Scott's. Reputedly as a result Mrs. Scott never spoke to Mrs. Whitaker again.

Brought up in the horse-show ring, Marian had a very high standard of conformation in her mind. I bought many horses for her, without her seeing them, with a fair amount of success. One mare bred a horse who was fancied for the Kentucky Derby when he broke both forelegs in an accident and could not be saved for stud. I also found a horse called Herons Plume for her from Fred Rimell's stable. He won easily at Saratoga but broke down. Afterwards she kept him at stud to breed hunters and steeplechasers.

When Marion Scott died, there was sadly, a family dispute about the will. But in the end, Montpelier and its park were left to the equivalent of the National Trust of America and both are open to the public. She also endowed for a very large sum an equine research station at Morven University in Virginia and made it over with funds to the university. I was asked to speak at the opening ceremony but sadly was already unable to travel.

If you are in America and have a few days to spare between the skyscrapers of New York or Broadway and the beaches it would be worth a trip to Virginia to see the autumn leaves turn to an unbelievable carpet of beauty. Look first at the view from the steps below Montpelier across the park to the woods and the Blue Ridge mountains beyond. Then go inside and look over the paintings, mainly cock fighting oils and the furniture of both European and Colonial style. Or, if you prefer, spend some time in the trophy room surrounded by cups and photographs of great wins. When you leave it will be nearly dark. So, go round the house to the formal gardens laid out with box hedges. There I am sure you will see a little old lady clad in brown or grey, her skirts down to her ankles and her hat, of the "heath" variety, pulled down over her ears. In her arms or at her feet will be a border terrier by name of Wallis or — if Heaven is kind — a whole pack of border terriers squabbling and playing as they have at Montpelier over the years. If you go up to her and ask a question, she will answer "Yes" or "No" with no prevarication before she fades away into the Virginian dusk.

There were many other places and people in Virginia where hospitality abounded, including Mrs. Augustus, who had, with her daughter Peggy, a stud farm from which she consigned some of the top lots at Saratoga. She was an aunt of Danny Van Clief. There was Bill W. Haggin-Perry, who lived in Virginia, though he raced a large stable in California. Paul Mellon lives not far from Upperville in Virginia. Of all the pictures, I confess to remember best, not a well-known masterpiece, but a painting of hounds pursuing a fox over a roof.

Not far from here are the Graysons and Blue Ridge Farm, where Never Say Die was foaled. The stud was founded by Admiral Grayson, who was President Roosevelt's personal physician. It is said that for the last nine months of the President's tenure of office, he was too ill to attend to business and that the Admiral governed the country for him. One of the foundation mares of the Grayson's organization was a mare called Winkle, imported from England through the BBA. The farm is now owned by Admiral Grayson's sons, one of whom, Gordon, comes to England frequently, and, as a reward for Never Say Die, Blue Ridge Farm secured a nomination to the horse when he went to stud.

Gordon Grayson asked us to buy him a mare in England to go to the horse. Being a connoisseur of pedigrees, he agreed to buy a mare from one of Lord Derby's very best families. To Never Say Die, she produced a small chestnut filly, who was named Virginia Dare after the first white baby to be born in the state of Virginia. Despite such a distinguished name, she hardly grew at all and when in training with Peter Walwyn was only just over 15 hands. She could go a little bit but not quite enough and managed to be second, narrowly beaten at various places including Windsor, Chepstow and Ally Pally. She had a bit of a temperament and Peter, at 6 foot 2 inches, trying to saddle her at 15 hands, was an interesting sight. Although she did not win the Graysons bought her back to America where she bred two stakes winners, including Roanoke Island, now at stud and sire of nearly a dozen stakes winners. In some ways the Graysons were lucky. For instance, when I bought them a very moderate Tom Rolfe filly, called Acquisitor, who only managed to win at Carlisle, they woke up the next year to find her half-brother Tasso had become the leading two-year-old in U.S.A. — such is the luck of racing and breeding.

Virginia is not, of course the only State where horses are bred. I also visited Kentucky but so much has already been said about the acres of rolling blue grass (more green than blue!), the miles of fencing, the huge barns and the fabulous collection of stallions and mares. Some individuals, living in Kentucky will, however, come into the story later.

Before going there I feel bound to describe in some detail some of my friends elsewhere, starting in New Jersey. Joe Roebling, whose family had built a famous bridge near Trenton, lived in a large house surrounded by woods. As a result of falls playing polo, he had by the time I knew him become severely restricted in his movements ending up in a wheel chair propelled by his chauffeur Donald. He had horses in America and England for years, his first trainer in England being Gerald Balding with whom he played polo. Gerald trained for him a good sprinter in Power House, just beaten in the 1956 Portland Handicap. His small broodmare band, kept latterly in Kentucky, produced numbers of stakes winners. His best horse in America was probably Blue Peter who won the Flamingo and other good races. He also had a very good mare called Portage, who bred numerous stakes winners. I bought him a Grey Sovereign filly called Be Cautious whom I saw win at Lingfield. She was a great success on the racecourse in the States, winning a division of the Trent Stakes, and also of the Black Helen. But she was not a success at stud. He also had in Meissen a useful stayer in

50

England, who, trained by his godson, Ian Balding, won a couple of races at Ascot as a three-year-old in 1971 and as a four-year-old, ridden by Luca Cumani, the Moet and Chandon Silver Magnum at Epsom over the Derby course.

I was invited once to shoot at his New Jersey home. They had had a release of pheasants the previous week and this party was to clear up the survivors. There were four guns, all padded up with leather gaiters against thorn bushes. One of them was Anderson Fowler, a member of the Jockey Club, whose importance to the party was that he brought with him a pointer, a very well trained dog with a good nose but stone deaf. When he pointed, all the guns ran through the thorns in the hope of getting to the spot before the bird flew up. As it was 80 degrees we had a good sweat. I cannot remember what we got but all was due to the deaf pointer!

Not all the contacts in America came from inside the horse world. Several friends had been in Washington during the war and they recommended us particularly to the Freling-huysens, Harry and Marian. Harry's family had been bankers in New Jersey and New York for centuries and he was one hundred percent American; his great interests being American football, racing and jazz. His father had raced a small stable very much as a hobby and up to the time we met had never owned a stakes winner. Marian was not really interested in racing but lived a busy social life in Far Hills, New Jersey and New York as well as making frequent visits to Europe.

Harry asked me to find his father a stakes winner and partly with my help he obtained a Grey Sovereign filly who won a small "stake race" in Florida over four furlongs in January of her two-year-old career. Encouraged by this success they asked me to buy them a yearling in England by the same sire. I suggested that they would do better to buy a foal, so as to give him time to acclimatize — advice which I would still give today. So I was given the order for a foal at the 1958 December Sales. I chose a tough looking, strong individual, typical of his sire, Grey Sovereign, from a fairly good family.

51

He went to America where he was named Merry Ruler and was soon found to have the main faults of Grey Sovereign and his sons: he had a mind of his own. His trainer Eddie Yowell had him gelded and from then on he was no trouble and clearly very fast. Early in his three-year-old career he won the Swift Stakes and was third in the Gotham Stakes in New York, a preparatory race for the Kentucky Derby. But he did not have enough staying power for that race and became a top class sprinter instead, winning eight stake races. He was a horse who gave his owners much pleasure, doubly so as all doormen, chauffeurs and head waiters always asked after the horse as soon as they saw the owners, and Merry Ruler seldom let them down.

Encouraged by these successes we thought up an idea which would give equal pleasure to Harry and Marian. The plan was to buy a yearling filly in England who would after her racing career go to stud in Florida. The sire was obvious, no other than Grey Sovereign, successful twice already for the Frelinghuysens. The next problem was the trainer. Cecil Boyd-Rochfort was the first suggestion. He would have looked up Frelinghuysen (Kingsland) in the New York social directory and accepted Marian as an owner at once. But it did not seem to me that a one horse owner with definite ideas about when she wanted it to run would fit in at Freemason Lodge. So I plumped for Freddie (Maxie) Maxwell, then training at Lambourn with a stable of about thirty or forty horses. I knew he and Norah would fit in with Marian, and that he was a very good trainer.

When I was looking at yearlings at Newmarket in 1963 I came across a good strong sort of filly with great quarters and power from a winner-producing, but not classic family. There was only one doubt in my mind. She was broad in the chest. While I was inspecting her Jack Colling was standing near by. I asked him if he would ever buy a yearling broad in the chest. He answered without hesitation but clearly not without thought. "I would never buy a colt who was wide in the chest but I do not mind it in a filly, provided the legs are correctly set on."

52

Fortified by Jack Colling's advice I bought her for 3,000 guineas with, I hope the approval of Maxie. I say hope because he is not always entirely easy to understand. For instance his orders to jockeys often amazed me. One day a filly of the Frelinghuysens was running at Newbury. She was not much good but did win a race. Her problem was that she galloped with her head held very low. On this occasion, the apprentice due to ride was involved in a fall in the previous race and could not ride. The substitute appeared just as the jockeys were mounting, whereupon Maxie said "She is a nice filly, mind you keep her in front of you." With that he threw the boy up — good advice but not easy to work out!

Another time a good jockey was to ride a colt of theirs first or second time out. He arrived in the paddock as the jockeys were mounted and was told by Maxie "This horse is a gentleman. I want you to ride him like one." The correct interpretation of this remark was roughly "Give him a nice ride, but do not knock him about!"

The filly I bought for Marian was out of a mare of Mrs. George Lambton's breeding. She was named Merry Madcap and in the spring of her two-year-old career in 1964 ran first time out at Sandown. Ron Sheather, now training at Newmarket, rode her. In a field of twenty five or so, she was slowly away, made up a bit of ground and finished in the middle division. I walked up the hill thinking she had shown neither speed nor stamina and was amazed when her jockey said "This is a good filly, she will win next time." I thought he was putting it gently to the owner but when he repeated his remark to Maxie, I knew he meant it. How right he was! Ridden by Lester Piggott she won four that year and next year won the July Cup in the presence of her owner, who shouted her home with great enthusiasm. She was returned to their farm in Ocala but though her offspring sold well, they did not shine on the racecourse.

Although they never had many horses, not more than one or two at a time, the Frelinghuysens had a high proportion of winners. Marian would ring up Maxie and tell him the date of a fashionable wedding or christening in Europe. Maxie almost invariably produced a runner at that time and often a winner. One of those was Whirled, out of a mare called Petara I found for Harry. Whirled was good enough to run well in the 1967 One Thousand Guineas. She not only had a good record in England, being a winner at Ascot, but went to Deauville for the Prix de la Callone, which she won, giving great pleasure to Marian's Paris friends summering there. In her final race she was just beaten in the Prix de la Foret at Longchamp.

Marian was a tremendous traveller and came over for as many races as she could. Once she arrived at our home in Hampshire with a pack of followers. After the first course she had to be told to decide on food or racing. We drove to Newbury, where Maxie produced a filly, who naturally won comfortably. In the unsaddling enclosure, she said "I am off to Highclere to see 'Porchie' Carnarvon." She woke the old gentleman from his afternoon sleep and after a cup of tea went straight on to London Airport and Europe.

On another occasion in the summer of 1966 she came to Salisbury to see the Whistler colt she had called Whiffenpoof run and, of course, win. After the race the stewards kindly asked her to tea in the wooden hut perched up by the winning post. While they were all sitting round with that slightly bemused expression brought on by the presence of foreigners on some English faces, she said "I must find my jockey Jimmy Lindley a present. What does he like?" Someone said "Shooting". "What about a pair of Purdeys?" she suggested. There was silence. All the teacups descended to the table, except for the stewards' secretary. He swallowed his cup almost whole and rushed from the room to ask the ring inspector if there had been a fabulous bet on the winner. At last someone — I think it was the late Archie Kidston — recovered enough to say "Madam, the race was worth £1,500 not £15,000." "Oh," she said. "Then he can have a pair of Whiffenpoof cuff links." If you do not know what a Whiffenpoof looks like, ask Jimmy Lindley to show you his cufflinks.

The most dramatic occasion, however, was when Merry

Madcap was due to run at the Salisbury spring meeting of 1964. Marian flew over the night before and we met her in London. She was very puzzled because the *Evening Standard* did not show the filly as a runner for the following day. We rang up Maxie, whose wife said she had taken the declarations to Weatherbys herself. There was nothing we could do that night, though Marian was very upset that Harry should think she had come over on false pretences.

Norah Maxwell was not yet beaten. At 9 o'clock when Weatherbys office opened, she was there in person. "I put in the declaration for Merry Madcap myself in plenty of time and that is the man" she said, "who received it." Now the British Post Office, or British Rail, or British Airways would have told her to go away. But to give them their due, Weatherbys set up a search — and found the declaration correctly timed and stamped under a blotter. There was a quick reference to the rules of racing from which it appeared that she was entitled to run. Norah Maxwell telephoned Lester Piggott and Weatherbys told Salisbury Racecourse and the press. The appearance of Mrs. H.O.H. Frelinghuysen's Merry Madcap on the runners' board startled everyone, especially when the name L. Piggott was seen against it. The bookmakers suspected a "coup" and opened up by making her favourite but as there was no money for her, she soon went out to 100-8. This did not stop Lester from winning comfortably and the press having a bonanza. The talented artist Peter Biegel has painted the start of that race with Salisbury Cathedral in the background. Harry Frelinghuysen has a marvellous collection of Impressionists but, if there was a fire, that might well be the picture he would save.

The Frelinghuysens' run came to an end when some irregularities were found in the accounting department of the family firm and someone was found to have got away with a fortune. Being the man he is, Harry decided to sell his own personal stud to help make good the damage. I went over to Keeneland to see them sold, a sad occasion, though they sold for sums far in excess of what they had cost.

Oddly enough, as with so many dispersal sales, the horses hardly lived up to their reputations in new ownership.

I had been lucky for the Frelinghuysens and I had been lucky, in the same period, for an English friend of pre-war days — Andrew MacIlwaine. When I was at Oxford I bought a point-to-pointer through Andrew, a retired cavalry officer who had a successful horse-dealing business at Guilsborough in the Pytchley country. She had been a useful animal though a very hard puller. When we were approaching the last fence in the South Oxfordshire Open race upsides with the leader, I got too excited and managed to throw her down. When I woke up Willie Kelly, who kept her for me, was leaning over saying "Begorra, they're the both of them dead!" But he was wrong. I recovered and sold the mare to the West country where she gave Anthony Mildmay a fall which scarred his face for life.

I had hardly seen Andrew MacIlwaine since, until he rang me up and said "My rough-rider is retiring and I am cutting down on my hunter trade. I'd like a good, well-bred broodmare which I can see in the field from the window and I'll sell her foals. A good hunter can be had for £400, so you ought to be able to get me a good mare in foal for the same price."

I told him that £4,000 would hardly be enough but that I would try. For the first three days of the 1957 December Sales, I laboured for him and others but could find nothing in the £400 range. Just when I was despairing, I saw a mare which at first glance had some message for me. Looking up the catalogue, I found she was by Big Game out of the Nearco mare Nivea, a useful female line. She was barren, though her breeding record until then was good.

I thought I would see her sold. No one showed much interest and the mare Conceal was knocked down to some unidentified bidder for 45 guineas. A Big Game mare for 45 guineas and a young mare at that! I rushed round to where her new purchasers were standing looking at her, hoping neither of them would be wearing a butcher's apron. They turned out to be Welsh farmers. With the aid of an Anglo-

Welsh dictionary I declared my interest and after a long haggle bought her for 85 guineas. But who was she for? I knew my partners would not relish taking her on and, standing still among the Welshmen, I had to admit that she had pretty bent hocks. Yet there were two things in her favour: she was by Big Game and she was cheap.

After a lot of thought, I rang up Andrew MacIlwaine and said that I had a mare which he could have, if he wanted her. She was a good-fronted, good walking mare with bent hocks and she was barren. But she was by Big Game and she was cheap. The name of the sire rang some sort of a bell and the price pleased him. So, he agreed to buy. When he saw her he was horrified as a good hunting man should be at her hocks. I told him that she should not have to use them for jumping. He was unhappy. But he accepted her.

Instead of sending her to Newmarket to a commercial sire, he sent her to the nearest horse he could find, Woodcut, a Fair Copy horse, standing at the Chesterton Stud in Warwickshire at a fee of 48 guineas. Conceal duly got in foal and produced a filly. Jack Leader was a friend of Andrew's and he saw and liked this filly. He took her off the breeder and sold her for 900 guineas as a yearling to Commander Kenneth Grant and Lord Rotherwick, who called her Hidden Meaning. Running in Kenneth Grant's name Hidden Meaning showed as a two-year-old in 1961 that she was out of the ordinary by winning a couple of races at Newmarket and the Solario Stakes at Sandown. As a three-year-old she won Kempton's 1000 Guineas Trial early on, lost her form somewhat in the summer, but in spite of 9 stone on her back won the Cambridgeshire easily. The story is best told in *Racehorses of 1962* published by Phil Bull's Timeform organisation; essential reading, I think, for all racegoers. "On last Wednesday afternoon a solitary horseman was seen wending his way across Newmarket Heath" — a quotation from a Sunday paper which conveys the ease with which Hidden Meaning won the Cambridgeshire — the first favourite to score since Palais Royal II in 1928 and in a record field of 46. Hidden Meaning passed the post two lengths in front of the runner-up — a winning margin which gives no idea of her superiority.

Hidden Meaning's partners then sold her to the Duke of Norfolk for some £12,000 but her first four foals were of no account and in 1967 the Duke sold her in foal to Aureole to America where she had a daughter who has bred one or more stakes winners. Conceal herself continued to produce good foals to better stallions. They sold well for Andrew but none of them was worth a light on the racecourse. None of them had bad hocks. There is certainly as much luck as skill in breeding Cambridgeshire winners.

CHAPTER 5

Never Too Late

THE GREAT STALLION STATIONS, the miles of railed
paddocks, the huge barns of Kentucky have been described
too often for me to do so again. But I did have two friends in
Kentucky worth a mention.

One was Mrs. Walter Salmon, widow of the President of
Mereworth Farm, which she ran in conjunction with her
step-son Walter Salmon junior. I was given an introduction
to her by Lionel Cecil, then our insurance broker. She
thought the letter came from another Cecil — Sir Cecil
Boyd-Rochfort — and immediately asked me round to her
house in New York. The policy of Mereworth Stud was to
buy up "stakes winners" for the stud. As the system of
"black type" races and Group races, now universally
accepted, was not in existence then, I had to find her good
winning fillies. This allowed me to buy for her such fast
mares as Krakenwake, winner of the Molecomb at
Goodwood as a two-year-old in 1958 and third in the Kings
Stand the next year and Egualita, winner of the 1963 Ayr
Gold Cup. Most of these mares and fillies produced
commercial propositions for the Saratoga Sales and one, the
only one who was *not* a good winner turned out to be a half
sister to the Kentucky Derby winner Tomy Lea. Mrs.
Salmon eventually remarried. Warry Gillette was a hero of
the first world war, who had flown on our side before
America came into it. He was keen on steeplechasing and we
bought him a mare to run in the Grand National. I shall never
forget standing at the top of the stand at Aintree and
watching her not only complete the first circuit but run up
into fourth place four fences from home, when the inevitable
happened and she fell. By that time, no spectators in the
vicinity were watching the race, but were enthralled by the

antics and howls of Colonel Gillette as he cheered his mare to the ground.

A remarkable character who lived in Kentucky at Harrodsburg, some twenty miles from the centre of the blue grass country, was Pansy Parker Poe. She was born an Ireland and married Parker Poe, a direct descendant of Edgar Allan Poe. When this happened the coloured help on her farms said "Mr. Poe will not be po' no mo'!" He had little interest in the horses but it proved an abiding and successful marriage. Pansy Poe had many interests including the Shawnee Farm in Kentucky where she bred yearlings for sale at Keeneland and Saratoga. She also had racehorses in Ireland trained by Paddy Prendergast, of whom she was very fond. He did a marvellous job for her in buying young stock and generally timed her winners for the Royal Ascot meeting when she was often over here.

I bought some mares for her for the Saratoga yearling market and went several times to stay at her Shawnee Farm. There she had a rough area wired off and within these confines her private pack of foxhounds hunted, mainly at night. She also had a charming place in Florida on the borders of Georgia and when she moved there in the autumn, the hounds in a hound van went there too. She kept for many years a tame fox and when the move took place to Florida, it travelled in a kennel on top of the hound van — and returned in the same way in the spring. The house in Kentucky was a very attractive old building crammed with furniture of all sorts. When she went to Europe, as she did most years, the antique dealers reaped a great harvest.

Pansy Poe was a short figure, described once as rather like a round rubber ball. It was hard to believe that she had been a keen polo player. She was still very keen on shooting, which was the main reason for her having an estate on the Florida/Georgia borders. There was a good stock of quail on her land and she would have friends to stay for shooting parties. The procedure was for the guns to be mounted in carriages drawn by mules. They would follow the pointers or setters until they marked a covey. Then two "guns" would seize their Purdeys and walk up behind the dogs. When the covey exploded in all directions, they were not as easy to hit as you might think.

There were also wild turkeys on her land. They were looked after by what is known as a turkey sitter, a man whose sole job was to follow round the flock and "sit with them," keeping them, if he could, on her estate and driving away marauders. Two or three times a year they had a turkey shoot and the birds were driven over narrow rides in the forest. Despite their size they were not as easy to hit as all that, embracing great speed with a short skyline.

I was there in early March immediately after the shooting season when there were acres of camellias all in full flower and the climate was not too hot.

In 1965 Pansy Parker Poe won the Gimcrack at York with the Grey Sovereign colt Young Emperor, who was out of Young Empress, bred by David Hely-Hutchinson at his Orchardstown Stud. Parker agreed to deliver the speech at the dinner and Pansy asked me to write it. Unlike the usual line in violent criticism of the racing authorities, it contained little to amuse or arouse the press. But he delivered it beautifully.

The main speaker that year, other than the owner of the winner, was Sir Alec Douglas-Home (now Lord Home). After the dinner, we met up in Pansy Poe's rooms in the Station Hotel, York, and had a long discussion on the facts of life, between the two greatest experts in their own fields. I was not sure if Paddy Prendergast knew who Sir Alec was but the latter certainly had a great knowledge of racing which he endeavoured by talking to Paddy to improve.

Pansy Parker Poe and the Salmons were both based in Kentucky. I suppose my most satisfied, though hardly my most grateful clients, were Mr. & Mrs. Howell Jackson of the B ull Run Stud, Virginia. They came into my life through "Bull" Hancock of Claiborne, Kentucky, who usually dealt with Tom Cooper of BBA (Ireland). This time "Bull" told me that Mr. Howell Jackson wanted two or three of the best mares available. "Bull" had put up to him everything that he could find but none were accepted. I said that I would do my best and asked if, when I found something, I should come back to him. "No," he said "I don't want to hear any more about it." So I was on my own.

Before long I came across a mare called Gloria Nicky by Alycidon out of Weighbridge in foal to Never Say Die. Like her dam she had been a very good race mare, winning the 1954 Cheveley Park as a two-year-old and being rated the best filly of her age. She belonged to Mrs. Robert Digby and rumour that she was for sale turned out to be at least half true. I was told by Di Digby that I could offer her and duly did so. To my surprise the Howell Jacksons came back straight away and we were soon negotiating a price. From memory this was about 36,000 guineas — a very large sum in those days and I believe, in fact, then the world record price for an unproven brood mare.

Di Digby was very reluctant to sell but, despite her doubts, she stuck nobly to her word. As is now well known, Gloria Nicky foaled in 1957 a filly to be named Never Too Late, who was trained in France by Etienne Pollet. There she became a leading two-year-old and came over here at three to win both the 1000 Guineas and the Oaks. Her last appearance in England was in the Champion Stakes, where she was just beaten by the big Italian champion Marguerite Vernaut. She was "over the top" by then.

Never Too Late was small but a dark chestnut of great quality and a beautiful mover. Gloria Nicky's next foal was also a good race filly by Swaps called Fall In Love II, who won good races in France and was second in the 1964 Cheveley Park to Major L. B. Holliday's Night Off.

Before the arrival of Never Too Late, in fact shortly after we had bought Gloria Nicky, I heard through our agent in France, Marquis Antoine de Rose, that Monsieur Maurice Hennessy was considering selling his top class mare La Mirambule, second to Zabara in the 1952 1000 Guineas and later second in the Prix de l'Arc de Triomphe. I immediately rang up Howell Jackson in Virginia. He showed interest and asked for her particulars to be sent to him. They were despatched at once : but for weeks I heard nothing from the Jacksons. We had promised Mr. Hennessy that the mare would not be "hawked." So I was getting very anxious when suddenly one Sunday Howell rang up and said "I want that mare." Apparently Mrs. Jackson found the particulars on her husband's desk and said "Get on quickly, Howell, buy that mare." But what could have been done easily a month before was now difficult. Antoine de Rose intercepted Mr. Hennessy on his way to the National Hunt Meeting at Cheltenham. He had by then given up the idea of selling his great mare. But being a man of his word, he agreed to go through with the deal.

La Mirambule bred for Howell Jackson, Nasram II, who won the 1964 King George and Queen Elizabeth Stakes at Ascot from Santa Claus and she also bred Tambourine II, who won the 1962 Irish Derby — the first of the new style well-rewarded Irish Derbys which put the race firmly on the classic map. For at least another fifteen years Howell had a large private stable in France and professed to be on the look-out for good mares. But he never bought another one through me. I should have thought that to provide him with the winners of three classics and the King George VI and Queen Elizabeth Stakes from only two mares, might have inclined him to dip again into the same bucket. But he did not do so.

Never Too Late was not the only Oaks winner with which I was connected. Doreen Margetts, a client of mine who divided her life between British Columbia and New Zealand, sent me a list of mares in the 1959 December Sales of which she would want one. Top of the list was the 13-year-old mare Duke's Delight, submitted as part of a reducing operation by the Stanhope Joel's Snailwell Stud at Newmarket. I liked this mare and had her vetted in the usual way. She was in foal to Lord Derby's Mossborough. Doreen Margetts, who had chosen her on paper, was very keen to have her. So we bid and got her for 1500 guineas. She duly foaled a small but well made filly, who was entered for the December Sales whilst her dam went off to New

63

Zealand. She had a reserve of either 3,000 guineas or 4,000 guineas on her as a foal and, believe it or not, no one would buy her. After consultation, we decided to keep her in England instead of sending her to New Zealand to re-submit her as a yearling.

When she came up at Newmarket our men who looked after her told me that hardly anyone had come to see her. As I was leaving her box I had the luck to run into Paddy Prendergast, that great judge and buyer of yearlings. I told him about her and recommended her to him. He said he had not got time to see her then but he marked his catalogue and when she came into the ring he bought her for only 4,200 guineas. She was named Noblesse and became one of the better Oaks winners of her era.

Another filly whom I bought was probably an unlucky loser of the Oaks. Sir John (Jakie) Astor, a friend from Oxford and Bullingdon days, told me at the end of the 1970's that he had cut down his stud in numbers and hoped to retain just two or three top-class mares. At that moment he was rather short of ammunition and needed to race a filly which might be good enough to retain. It was between sales times and after a long search my French partner Count Bernard de Saint Seine told me of a yearling filly by Green Dancer out of the Charlottesville mare Khazaeen. After negotiation we bought her — not cheaply. Named The Dancer, she proved herself in 1979 a good two-year-old, beating Mrs. Penny, future winner of the Cheveley Park, on her debut at Newbury, and beating a field of note at Doncaster on St. Leger day. It was thought worth while therefore to send her to Longchamp for the Criterium des Pouliches on Prix de l'Arc de Triomphe day. In this she ran disappointingly and on return to Dick Hern's stable was given a check up by the stable vet. It was found that she was going blind in one eye.

As a three-year-old The Dancer was fitted with a contraption covering the blind eye and, as she went well at home, she continued racing. She won a listed race, the Sir Charles Clore Memorial Stakes at Newbury in May, making practically all the running, and when the Oaks came it was thought that the best tactics would be to try to lead all the way again. Willie Carson was on Dick Hollingsworth's home bred Bireme, Ernie Johnson rode The Dancer. The Astor filly ran a gallant race. She coped with Epsom's twists and turns, uphill and downhill, until the hill down to Tattenham corner where she hesitated but soon recovered and ran on to be third, beaten two lengths and a short head by Bireme and the Bruce Hobbs trained Vielle.

Another successful classic filly with whom I was concerned was Enstone Spark. One day in 1977 my partner Brian Gething told me that he had seen a very nice Sparkler filly for sale at Richard Hannon's yard at East Everleigh in Wiltshire. She had won three races fairly early in the season and he was keen to buy her for the West Indies. I went over to see her and, like Brian, fell in love with a small, all quality filly with tremendous quarters, a great walker and a June foal. While I was extolling her virtues she won the Lowther Stakes at York thereby putting her beyond the reach of the West Indies. She belonged to a man of a certain age who had lost his sight. He felt he had to sell. I told a Canadian, Dick Bonnycastle, about her and he asked me to buy her to race for two more races and then send her to the American coast — in fact to California, to race there. The price was from memory between 25,000 and 30,000 guineas. One of Dick's friends, a racing paper proprietor at that, told him and everyone else that he had paid far too much. But she had already won the Lowther Stakes and to my mind was good value.

Before Enstone Spark could fly to California, a ban was imposed on all imports from over here. So Dick decided to race her here and to send her to his own trainer, Barry Hills at Lambourn. This was meant as no disrespect to Richard Hannon, who had trained her so well.

Barry soon realized that she was a good filly and told us to back her for the 1978 1000 Guineas — her first race of the season. I think my wife was one of the few people to take his advice at 66/1. Ridden by Johnson, Enstone Spark won the 1000 Guineas nicely from Fair Salinia and Seraphima, despite coming off a straight line. On that day she was a very good

65

filly indeed. Fair Salinia, trained by Michael Stoute, went on to win the Oaks, the Irish Oaks and the Yorkshire Oaks in succession to emphasise the form.

Enstone Spark next ran at Ascot in the Coronation Stakes, where she fell on the home turn. She never recaptured her form after that and was retired to Canada, where she bred Dick Bonnycastle a filly or two before he sold her for over 600,000 dollars.

One of my less successful buys as a racehorse for Dick Bonnycastle was Goosie Gantlet, a filly by Run The Gantlet from the Sea Bird II mare Goosie, bred at the Dalham Hall Stud at Newmarket. She came from a great family but hardly lived up to her breeding, although Barry did win a race with her as a three-year-old at Redcar in 1977. She was thought not to be good enough to send to Canada and so consigned to the December Sales. But before she went up she was discovered to be a very bad crib-biter. She would only have been sent back if sold at Newmarket and so Dick passed her on to a friend, Alan Boone, his partner in his publishing business. Although she ate fences, she has nearly always got in foal and has been a good winner producer, including Rikki Tavi, who won the Ascot Stakes in 1980.

While Dick Bonnycastle was on the whole a lucky owner, there was at least one occasion when he was not. He used to enjoy the Irish yearling sales at Kill and liked to buy there. One September day in 1981 he said he was coming and gave us the flight number of his aircraft. On the day of the sale, we sent off a car to the airport and Barry Hills and I looked out a few yearlings. We had been told that he wanted three or four. The sale began with no sign of Dick Bonnycastle. After a bit we decided to buy two or three, which he could see when he arrived. We had bought three nice horses and were looking over our shoulder for Dick when a bay filly by Home Guard came into the ring. It was her walk that took the eye. Nobody seemed much interested and the auctioneer was looking around with more hope than expectation when we made our bid of 10,000 Irish punt which happened to be the reserve, so that she was knocked down to the BBA. At almost

1. Robin and Jean Hastings at Mexico City Racecourse in 1955.
2. Robin on his first pony, Polly, with his father the Hon. Osmond Hastings.
3. Robin, aged eight, at his Gloucestershire home.

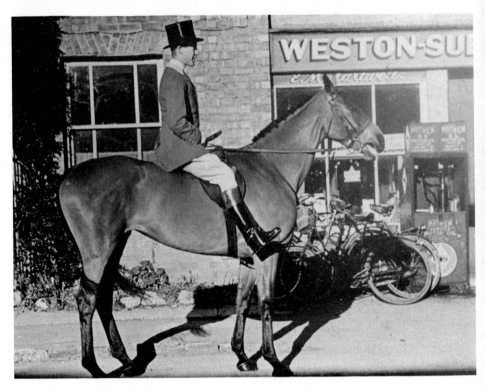

4. Robin out hunting with the North Cotswold in 1938.

5. Robin (left) at Stratford-upon-Avon on Chatmo beating Brian Marshall and P. J. Doyle in 1948.

6. Robin at the last hurdle at Doncaster before winning on Eight Reigns in 1948.

7. Mr A. V. Tabor (bowler hat) about to lead in Eight Reigns.

8. Robin (right) winning at Leicester on Monk's Crest in 1950 from
Colonel Billy Smith — first ride after broken collarbone.
9. Jean Hastings and Rupert in 1951 – two reasons for leaving the army.

10. Merry Madcap (Lester Piggott up) at Salisbury in 1964, by Peter
Biegel.

11. Mrs Scott and her dogs.

12. The late Danny Van Clief's Unbiased with Geoffrey Brooke and Doug Smith.

13. Never Too Late winning the 1960 Oaks from Paimpont and Imberline.

14. Nasram II, winning the 1964 King George VI and Queen Elizabeth Diamond Stakes at Ascot from the Derby winner Santa Claus.
15. Robin and Brigadier R. A. Scott at Newmarket, 1971.

16. Shirley Heights (on the left) winning the 1978 Derby from Hawaiian Sound.

17. Petoski going to the post in the 1985 King George IV and Queen Elizabeth Diamond Stakes at Ascot (W. Carson up).

that moment the car driver came back with no news of Mr. Bonnycastle on any flight and shortly afterwards Dick rang up to say that he was in a business wrangle, could not get over and did not want any yearlings. I said " You have already got four!" He said "Well, pass them on. Of course if you can't sell them, I'll take them."

Barry found owners in his yard for three immediately but no-one wanted the Home Guard filly who was out of a useful mare called Geraldville, who had won races for the McGillycuddys. Finally I decided to take her over myself to give to my wife, as a reward for enduring the life of a blood-stock agent for so long.

When I joined the BBA there was a rule that we did not own horses ourselves so that there would be no conflict of interest. It was not strictly enforced since Gerald McElligott at one time — but not for long — owned both Royal Charger and Tulyar. Under the more relaxed rule of R. Hastings, one or two wives had a horse or two. These very occasionally included Jean.

At one Ballsbridge in September 1960, which I ill-advisedly allowed Jean to attend, she fell in love with a distinctly crooked filly by Polly's Jet and while I was sitting on her hands preventing her bidding, Freddie Maxwell bought the filly for one hundred guineas. As luck would have it Jean sat next to him in the plane going home and by the time London Airport was reached she had bought half the filly for the auction price. This filly, Polly Macaw, a useful plater, was in the frame a number of times and won twice for us. On the second occasion at Wolverhampton in May 1961, I was not present as I was meeting an American client off the boat at Southampton. To our surprise there was a lot of bidding for her and finally at over 600 guineas Maxie said "That is enough." She was knocked down to Bob Ward. When he got her home and saw her legs he offered to let us have her back. But we refused.

Ward did well with her, winning four more sellers, but finally ran her at Lincoln the following May in a seven horse seller. She was ridden by Peter Robinson and backed down to favouritism. Bob Ward also had Ione in the race, ridden by Lester Piggott. Ione had opened in the betting at odds on but eased in the betting. Polly Macaw won by twenty lengths from Ione — a result which was to be expected from the betting and which resulted in a good old row. Bob Ward lost his licence and Lester was stood down for a while.

When Bob Ward tried to dispose of the filly he found no takers until an Irishman from Co. Meath offered him £400. For this man she bred a useful winner in Pollygaze immediately. After being barren in 1965, she was booked the next year to a local horse who died in the middle of the season. The man was scratching his head over what to do at this late stage when the hounds, with the master, Major Elwes, came past his house. In the course of conversation he put his problem to the master. Elwes suggested: "Why not send her to Hard Tack? He is only a field away."

The owner took the advice, sent the mare to Hard Tack and produced Right Tack, winner of both the English and the Irish 2,000 guineas in 1969. This was a lesson perhaps to all those from Signor Tesio through Madame Veuillier and Miss Alex Scrope on how to arrange matings!

So when we were left with the Home Guard filly on that September day in 1981, I eventually decided to give her to my wife, as I have already mentioned. Penny Hills took part of her and all would have been well if some American friends, the Jeffords, had not come over and agreed to take a share in her.

Jean called her Fenny Rough after a covert on her father's land in Worcestershire where there was always a litter of cubs. The filly's first claim to distinction was that she bucked and kicked and landed on top of a car.

This delayed her appearance as a two-year-old in 1982 until Kempton in mid-July. Barry was very busy elsewhere but the two English partners were present and Steve Cauthen brought her home by four lengths. Next time out she was fourth in the Princess Margaret Stakes at Ascot and then narrowly beaten in August at Salisbury, where she got a sod of earth up her nostril. She was then consigned to Pontefract,

where we thought the opposition would be less formidable.
On arrival at Pontefract, however, the first person we saw
was Peter Burrell plus Henry and Julie Cecil. So I thought we
should go straight home, for Henry's runner Concorde Hero,
the favourite, had already won at Newmarket, whilst others
with winning form were Domynsky of Peter Easterby's and
Johnny Nobody. Nonetheless Fenny Rough won well. The
second and third were both sold to America where they won
stakes races. So I knew ours was more than useful.

The next year Fenny Rough began as before by charging a
motorcar, and until July only amassed training bills. Barry
took her once to Newmarket to gallop but it was not until
the Goodwood July Meeting that she could run, in the Oak
Tree Stakes over seven furlongs on Stewards' Cup day.
The opposition was formidable. It included the favourite,
Silverdip, bred by George Strawbridge in America and
trained by Ian Balding. She had run well in the French 1000
guineas and had won a "listed" race for three-year-old
fillies at Newmarket earlier in the month. Lester Piggott was
on another recent winner Pig Tail, and Joe Mercer on Linda's
Fantasy, who had been a very good two-year-old, winning
five off the reel. Fenny Rough, ridden by Steve Cauthen, ran
a marvellous race, got the better of a long duel with Silverdip and won by a length to the great joy of all concerned.

Five weeks later Fenny Rough appeared at York in the
Strensall Stakes against another field of three-year-old
fillies, who again included Silverdip. This time Steve could
not get out to challenge when he wanted, and although Fenny
Rough was flying at the finish, Silverdip had got first run and
held on to win by half a length.

Fenny Rough only ran once more for us in Ireland at the
Curragh when she did not shine. But by then the offers were
coming in for her from various directions and when Robert
Sangster suggested he would buy her for £100,000 Jean and I
had to accept. The Jeffords sold out too, but Penny Hills
stayed in.

In California Fenny Rough immediately made her mark.
After winning an allowance race and a Group III stake, she

looked like being a real money-spinner. Robert Sangster was in America but on the east coast when someone rang up and asked if he would sell Fenny Rough. "No," he said, "certainly not."

"What about half a million dollars?"

"Well that's different. I suppose I shall have to say yes."

Having put the telephone down it rang again. It was John Gosden from California to tell him that Fenny Rough had just won a "stakes race." He was sad to lose her and forecast correctly that they would soon break her down — which they did. No filly gave her owners more pleasure and as far as I went her sale price almost paid for the wedding of our daughter Lucinda.

Standing in the same place at Kill the next year, Barry picked out a Lord Gayle filly walking well but with a definite tendency to turn her near fore in. I nodded my head once and the auctioneer knocked her down for 10,000 punt. As a two-year-old this Lord Gayle filly, now named Desirable, won the Princess Margaret Stakes at Ascot and later the Cheveley Park, beating Pebbles and most of the other top class fillies of her age. As a three-year-old she was sold at Newmarket for one million guineas. I was offered a share in Desirable but my Bank Manager would hardly have approved!

I have mentioned many friends on the other side of the Atlantic in this chapter — the Walter Salmons, the Parker Poes, the Howell Jacksons, Dick Bonnycastle, "Bull" Hancock, Doreen Margetts, and the Jeffords. Perhaps as a tailpiece I may tell of an American friend — a charming fellow by the name of Bowers. Humphrey Finney wrote and asked us to show him round the English studs. He did not think Bowers would be a buyer. He lived in Kentucky and was one of those Americans who had come into the war early, driving an ambulance to help our side. For that alone I made a special effort to take him round.

When he returned to the USA he wrote and thanked me for showing him Newmarket and said that in return he had made me a Kentucky Colonel, a charity organization which raises funds for good causes including police charities in the state. So I have in my downstairs lavatory alongside pictures of the Bullingdon in the 1930's a scroll declaring that I am a Kentucky Colonel. If you are one of these, it is as well in the State of Kentucky to carry your membership card, because its production is even more effective in helping the police not to prosecute than an Irish driving licence or passport!

The scroll had not long been installed, when I received another letter. Mr. Bowers was glad I had accepted the Kentucky Colonel's badge and wondered if in return I would ask the Queen to make him an OBE. Regretfully I declined!

CHAPTER 6

Shirley Heights

THERE IS PERHAPS no living American to whom racing in England is more in debt than Paul Mellon who, as most people will remember, won the 1971 Derby with Mill Reef, trained for him at Kingsclere by Ian Balding, who married my cousin Emma Hastings Bass.

Mill Reef was an outstanding racehorse, winning not only the Derby, but the Prix de l'Arc de Triomphe, the King George VI and Queen Elizabeth Stakes, the Eclipse Stakes, the Coronation Cup, the Gimcrack, and half a dozen other races. It will be remembered that he fractured a bone in his leg as a four-year-old and it seemed doubtful if he would ever be able to stand at stud and the vets did really well to save him.

Paul Mellon has a much bigger horse breeding enterprise in Virginia, where he has about fifty mares, than he does in Britain where only a dozen mares are based.

Mill Reef having been saved for the stud, Mellon very generously decided to stand the Derby winner in England at a far lower price than he could have got if he had flown his great horse back to the United States.

I was on holiday in Minorca when Mill Reef was considered to have recovered enough from his leg injury to go to stud. Ian Balding rang me up and asked me to go to New York the next day to discuss syndication over here with Mellon. I said "No, not unless you provide me with a new wife of equal value!" However, I did drag my wife out of the sea a week later and returned home. I flew out to New York overnight, discussed the syndication, recommended our National Stud, drafted the syndicate agreement and returned on the evening flight.

It so happened that amongst Paul Mellon's many English

friends were the late Lord Halifax and his wife. They both used to go and stay with him in Virginia and see his bloodstock at Rokeby. Paul Mellon invested in one of the Halifax mares at the time, the families remained close friends, and when Mellon generously decided to stand Mill Reef at the National Stud he wrote to Lord Halifax offering him a share in Mill Reef for £50,000.

Lord Halifax felt that he had no suitable mare to send to Mill Reef and decided that he must buy one. Lady Halifax at the time was already aware of her husband's health problems and saw that they would eventually curtail his favourite pastime of hunting the Middleton hounds from his home at Garrowby in Yorkshire. She got in touch with me and said that they wanted to find a suitable mare for Mill Reef and she wanted to buy a mare, too. We went through the 1973 December Sales catalogue and came up with a short list.

Finally we bought two mares, one beautifully bred and well conformed, who turned out to be very little good, the other a Hardicanute mare, heavy in foal, called Hardiemma, whom Lady Halifax had seen racing in the north. Hardiemma, trained by Jack Ormston at Richmond in Yorkshire, had won as a two-year-old and had been just beaten in the Beeswing Handicap at the Northumberland Plate meeting at Newcastle before winning a competitive handicap at Ayr. She was useful and genuine and was out of a mare called Grand Cross, who bred a total of eleven winners.

Apart from the fact that she was genuine it also appealed to Lord and Lady Halifax that Hardiemma's female line was full of winners — Grand Cross eleven winners, her second dam Blue Cross three, and the third dam King's Cross ten, including the top class miler King's Bench.

We went through the usual routine, having her out, examined by the vet and inquiries put out among those who knew her better than ourselves. She was knocked down to Lord Halifax and his only son, the then Lord Irwin, for 12,000 guineas, in foal to Upper Case.

Hardiemma was to prove an inspired purchase. Unfortunately her first foal by Upper Case called Hit The

73

Roof was only a selling plater, was small and showed no promise at all in her three runs as a two-year-old in 1976. Hardiemma was used to fill Lord Halifax's nomination to Mill Reef in 1974 and she went to the National Stud's other Derby stallion Blakeney in 1975.

The Mill Reef Hardiemma foal, Shirley Heights, was small and not particularly good looking as a yearling and the Blakeney filly foal Bempton was also small, nothing out of the ordinary. Lord and Lady Halifax decided to sell Hardiemma at the December Sales of 1976 in foal again to Mill Reef, knowing that they would have in due course Hardiemma's daughter Bempton for their stud.

I remember there was some discussion about the reserve on Hardiemma. I said that it should be at least the same as the fee for Mill Reef — then 15,000 guineas — and this was agreed. A Brazilian bid to 14,500 guineas and the auctioneer was just about to give up, when an Irishman, Ted Naughton, Manager of the Ballyrogan Stud, made one bid.

He secured for 15,000 guineas the dam of the future Derby winner Shirley Heights and the stud was to sell the full sister to Shirley Heights as a yearling in 1978 for 250,000 guineas! She was to prove of little account on the racecourse.

Sadly Lord Halifax was not to live long enough to see Shirley Heights make good as a stallion. He died just before the start of the 1980 flat racing season when the first Shirley Heights had just been foaled. Oddly enough Shirley Heights was not overwhelmingly popular when he went to stud at Sandringham but after getting two Derby winners things changed and a quick attempt at valuing the mares going to him in 1986 came out at £36 million!

Another friend of mine, Julian Byng, whom I met shooting grouse in Yorkshire, was also involved in Shirley Height's Derby. His host, Lord Bolton, had a horse or two in France and extolled the advantages of racing there. Julian Byng took this all in and decided to ask me to buy him a yearling or two. The first, a filly called Laughing Goddess by Green God out of Gay Baby, cost us 4,000 guineas as a yearling in 1974 and won her very first race, the Prix de Debut in Paris, and two races in England as a three-year-old before breeding him three or four winners.

Another purchase for 5,500 Irish Guineas was Pyjama Hunt who won six races and £141,250. As a two-year-old in 1977 he was an unlucky loser of the Grand Criterium when his young jockey found himself sandwiched between Yves Saint-Martin and Lester Piggott and went down by three quarters of a length. He was also unlucky in Shirley Heights's Derby. He was ridden by Gibert, who did not know Epsom. I foolishly told him that horses roll inwards up the hill at Epsom when tiring and that the rails were consequently a dangerous place. He therefore pulled him out to the centre of the course, lost his action for a few strides and then ran on to be fourth behind Shirley Heights, Hawaiian Sound and Remainder Man. I think that with a better run he could have been third. Julian Byng now has a stud and breeds his own horses with a certain amount of success.

Long before I met Julian Byng, I was closely associated with a friend of Oxford days, Tony Samuel, who was encouraged by me to take an interest in bad habits such as racing. Tony Samuel, after riding his own point-to-pointers before the war, started to breed his own flat racers afterwards. The best of these was Gilles de Ritz who won the 1956 2000 Guineas. He also bred the Grey Sovereign colt Raffingora, whom he was unable to sell as a yearling. He won for him as a two-year-old in 1967 at Epsom and at Goodwood. He had a very disappointing three-year-old career due partly to the cough in the stable. He gave him away for 2,700 at the end of his three-year-old season, whereupon he became one of the fastest sprinters in training. At the same time he decided to disperse his Eveton Stud and sold nearly all his mares. However, to keep an interest in racing he used to get me to buy a yearling for him every now and then. One of these turned out to be almost my favourite horse.

At the 1965 Dublin sales I came across a small all-quality colt by Proud Chieftain out of Oweninny, already dam of three winners. Geoffrey Brooke approved of him, we bought

75

him for 2,900 guineas, and Tony named him Owen Anthony.

As he was small, Geoffrey got him ready for the first flat race meeting of the season at Doncaster, when he thought he would win the Brocklesby. Unfortunately, he was slowly away and failed to oblige. But he made up for it by winning three times as a two-year-old.

Owen Anthony's three-year-old season in 1967 was a disappointment, owing to some sort of virus in the yard. He ran well a few times but did not win. The problem then arose of whether to sell him or keep him on for his four-year-old year. We decided to keep him on.

It was a lucky decision. Dropped in the handicap a few pounds, due in reality to the virus, he was established at an official weight from which he could win. Geoffrey Brooke retired and Tony Samuel gave Doug Smith the chance of training him. He was Doug's very first runner as a trainer and duly won an apprentice race at Doncaster on the first day of the 1968 season. He settled down to be a game and consistent handicapper, winning a total of eleven races, including the Newbury Spring Cup and the City and Suburban. He was placed many times in good handicaps but could not quite win the Royal Hunt Cup, in which he was once second, beaten narrowly by his half brother, and once close-up fourth. He always ran a good and genuine race and was practically never a disappointment to his owner.

When Owen Anthony was nine it seemed only fair to retire him and I found a stud near Billingshurst in Sussex who were prepared to take him. He bred a fair number of winners there but was not considered big enough to be used on the local steeplechase mares to produce jumpers. In fact, he has sired a useful number of jumping winners. I found a home for him in the West Country and then in Leicestershire with Derek Leslie, where he still covered a few mares until his death in January 1987.

In his early days at stud Owen Anthony was used by John Baillie who had a more than useful collection of mares not far away. One mare he sent to him called Luckhurst bred him Stumped, a good winner who earned enough black type to interest an American breeder. She went to America, being sent to Nureyev, where she produced none other than the outstanding filly Sonic Lady. So the name of gallant, little Owen Anthony will be inscribed forever in the Hall of Fame.

When Peter Walwyn began training in 1961 he sometimes used to ask me to help him in buying yearlings. In this connection, he introduced me to David Oldrey who, at that time was most interested in buying potential stayers. From then on we have had a happy and successful co-operation beginning with buying the stayer Crozier for 950 guineas in 1964. He was the winner of twelve races in England including the 1967 Doncaster Cup and the Grand Prix de Vichy in France.

Naturally Peter Walwyn has nearly always been present. Generally, but not always, David Oldrey has been there too. As is well-known, Oldrey has sufficient eye and knowledge to buy for himself. The common denominator has been myself. David became the owner of such horses as another Doncaster Cup winner Wagoner, bought as a foal for 7,000 guineas, as well as the 1985 Ascot winner Plaid. But the one who came nearest to classic success was Oats. He came from an early crop of Northfields, a son of whom I had bought for Lady Beaverbrook to win at Royal Ascot. Oats was not an expensive purchase. Having won Epsom's Blue Riband Trial Stakes, he proved himself worth a run in the 1976 Derby. Unfortunately, the blacksmith pricked him just before his last work for the race and he went to Epsom just short of a gallop to finish close up third to Empery and Relkino, beaten three lengths and a head. Without that misfortune, he might have held a higher place in the affections of mare owners, though he proved his merit as a four-year-old, winning his only three races.

Now that Mr. Stavros Niarchos has such a vast and successful stable, managed for many years by Sir Philip Payne-Gallwey, one is apt to forget his short foray into racing thirty years ago. He then asked my partner Brigadier Scott to find him a trainer and a horse or two. The very first one we bought was Oleandrin who was in Harvey Leader's

Newmarket stable. He won the Craven Stakes for him and was third to Nearula and Bebe Grande in the 1953 2000 Guineas, for which Mr. Niarchos had a nice bet each way at 60-1.

Mr. Niarchos met Sir Gordon Richards in Switzerland and decided to train with him, too. One of his buys was Pipe of Peace picked out by the Brigadier. He was a very good two-year-old in 1956, winning the Middle Park at Newmarket, ridden by Scobie Beasley. Next spring he won the Greenham, started favourite for the 2000 Guineas, and was beaten half a length and a head by Crepello and Quorum.

The Derby came next. Breasley had not long been in England. In Australia no jockey, if he is "off," ever leaves the rails and so when Pipe of Peace came into the straight at Epsom in the Derby Scobie kept right on the inside rail. At Epsom, because of the slope away from the stands, tiring horses, as I have said, tend to drift to their left. Pipe of Peace got the full weight of others coming over on top of him. He was again third, only beaten one and a half lengths and a length by Crepello and Ballymoss. Scobie always thought he might have nearly won if he had known Epsom better.

After the Derby Pipe of Peace rather lost his form. The reason, which Gordon Richards confided to us privately, was that he had begun to make a noise. Knowing this, it was hard for the BBA to recommend him as a stallion. Another intrepid agent George Forbes, however, stepped in. Gordon had him down on a windy day to his yard at Whitsbury near Salisbury and perhaps stood him with the wind behind as the horses went past. George detected nothing and bought him for a large sum for New South Wales where his defect was not passed on to his offspring and he was a huge success. Wind infirmities are in fact of no consequence in some dry climates, such as Australia and Argentina. I could mention, but perhaps had better not, several stallions in such places who, although themselves unsound in their wind, did not pass it on.

One of the people with whom I was able to do business and to have fun was Herbert Blagrave. He had been lucky enough to inherit a fair proportion of the town of Reading and was able to enjoy a life of fun and games. He played cricket for Gloucestershire, hunted and shot, and settled down in Wiltshire at Beckhampton where he trained his own horses, frequently using the fabulous gallops made famous by Fred Darling and more recently by Jeremy Tree.

Over the years Herbert trained a good number of winners at Ascot including three Royal Hunt Cups with Couvert and Master Vote (twice) but he never won the Ascot Gold Cup, though he bred the 1950 Ascot Gold Cup winner Supertello. He had a stud in Ireland, so that most of his horses were home-bred. But he had success over the years in buying horses in France, such as Atout Maitre and Legend of France. He also had the Harwood Stud near Newbury where he normally stood a stallion or two.

He used to get great enjoyment from taking a shoot and inviting his friends, finally buying Linkenholt, a marvellously wild, hilly estate near the north west corner of Hampshire, where the birds flew well. He kindly asked me often and my only hesitation about going there was that lunch always took so long that I had a dreadful feeling that it would be too dark to continue when the last port and brandy had been sunk.

Herbert was always proud of his Harwood Stud which has stood great horses such as Gainsborough, for whom it had originally been built by Lady James Douglas. He always talked of reviving its glories and one day he actually came round to taking steps to do so, asking me to help him find a top-class horse. As he had done well with French imports, he thought immediately of finding something there. Herbert Blagrave, like many other rich men by inheritance, was surrounded by hangers-on and frequently approached by people wanting money. He was, therefore, not inclined to overspend or indeed to make up his mind to sign the cheque at all. So one or two people who knew I was charged with finding him a horse, wished me luck and had a bet that I would not succeed.

The horse we picked on was Match III, a top-class middle

distance horse in France, and winner as a four-year-old in 1962 both of the King George VI and Queen Elizabeth Stakes at Ascot and of the Washington D.C. International at Laurel Park, from the great American horse Kelso.

Match III was owned and bred by Mons. Francois Dupre and trained by Francois Mathet. We went over to see Match — a trip enlivened by Herbert's command of French, learnt during the first world war in the trenches and in the estaminets behind the lines. We liked the horse, who was fine, strong and well-made but, perhaps lacking a little quality about the head. We then launched into endless negotiations. French trainers are entitled to a percentage on sales of horses from their yards, and this percentage has to be found by the owner. Consequently the trainers are out to make as much from the sale as possible. Francois Mathet from whose various yards I bought many horses, employed a particularly effective technique to squeeze the last franc from the deal. When the transaction had been virtually completed and the vet already en route to examine the horse, he would put the price up even further. This ploy almost always succeeded.

Match stood for three seasons at Herbert's stud and attracted a good book of mares. One morning, however, at eight o'clock the telephone rang. It was Herbert Blagrave's voice "We have lost Match, " he said. Apparently he had had some internal trouble and despite an urgent call for Dr. John Burkhardt to assist the regular vets, the horse died. Match sired a fair number of winners and was successful as a broodmare sire but he barely had time to set the world on fire.

Herbert was not to be defeated by this heavy loss. He came again to me and we decided to try to buy Reliance II, his own brother, at that time in 1965 unbeaten in France. He was a very different kettle of fish. A well-made strong bodied horse, he had extraordinary lop-ears and when you looked down at his fetlocks you found they were completely deformed so that his joints were almost on the ground. It was such a bad deformity that we came to the conclusion that it must have been caused by an accident at foaling, since he was certainly a good enough racehorse.

Herbert decided to take the risk and after the usual spell of bargaining, we bought him subject to various conditions for delivery after his four-year-old career during which time Francois Mathet was to train him.

At that time Francois Mathet had an arrangement with a veterinary expert in the South of France to operate on his really top-class horses to improve their performance. The idea was to re-cycle, as it were, their heartbeats. The heart would be stopped and re-started. He only tried this on a very few absolutely top class horses and whether it worked or not, I do not know. It was not doping and was within the Rules of Racing but it was dangerous practice.

Reliance II went there and was operated on. Unfortunately it did not work and, having stopped the heart, it proved impossible to restart it in a new rhythm. The horse nearly died and could not run again so came over to Herbert's stud to stand, an unfortunate affair for both horse and owner.

As a result of Match's death facilities at the stud were upgraded and a new team brought in, including a manager. Reliance became capable of covering something like a full book of mares and had reasonably good fertility. Few, if any, of his foals had bad forelegs and though their ability on the racecourse was limited on the whole, he produced some good racehorses and some very good broodmares. Unfortunately, the strains of his early troubles caught up with him and he died at an early age.

It could not be said that Herbert Blagrave was fully repaid for his enterprise nor that his efforts had a serious impact on British breeding. But they gave him some satisfaction and some fun, which was the main object of his life — whether it be from racing, shooting, having a good bet or just enjoying "laughter and the love of friends."

CHAPTER 7

South America

ONE OF THE CONSEQUENCES of the second world war was that the South American countries were cut off from Europe for five years. For the first half of the century and earlier, the upper classes in South America had sent their male children to be educated in England. Whether as a consequence of that or not, the predominantly Spanish families of wealth — or those of Portuguese extraction in Brazil — had developed an extraordinary interest in the English thoroughbred. In all sorts of places well away from Europe, you would find people who knew far more about our thoroughbred families than most Englishmen. Countries such as Argentina had been importing good class horses, including classic horses such as Bahram, Rustom Pasha and the war time Derby winner Pont l'Eveque. Even in those countries where there was no racing, there was an interest in English thoroughbreds despite the fact that there has been comparatively little racing in Spain.

After the war Brigadier Scott, who spoke Spanish well and had been busy in Argentina and elsewhere buying mules for the Far East during the war, re-visited most of the countries in South America and rekindled their interest in racing.

On his advice I followed in his footsteps without the same reputation or expertise or his knowledge of the language. Before the economic blizzard swept over the continent we helped to make up for the gaps in imports left by the war. I travelled therefore, a number of times to various countries in South America. In one memorable trip I took in Argentina, Brazil, Chile, Colombia, Peru and Venezuela.

Unlike the rest of the continent, Brazil had a Portuguese tradition and the inhabitants speak Portuguese. They had some sort of national affiliation with France and many of their imports came from that country, in the form of stallions and mares.

Because of the heavy rainfall, Brazil is a beautiful country with all sorts of tropical vegetation surrounding examples of Portuguese architecture. The capital Rio de Janeiro, when I went there — always for obvious reasons in February or March — was really too hot to enjoy. The sands on the Copacabana beach hurt one's feet. But San Paulo and the country around there was attractive and beautiful, though not the best place in the world to breed horses. You can breed horses anywhere in the world but there are only a few places where it can be done naturally, without excessive expense. Argentina, Chile, New Zealand, Kentucky, Normandy and parts of England and Ireland have natural advantages not shared by Brazil. But by importing fodder and additives the Brazilians were capable of producing some top-class racing stock.

We were lucky enough to acquire a very good agent in Samir Abujamra who has done a good business there for the last twenty years on our behalf. They imported some very good potential stallions and mares and even fillies for racing, while the country was prosperous. As it has every raw material imaginable, except for oil, it can only be a matter of time before it re-enters the prosperous section of the world.

On my first visit to Brazil I was invited to the Jockey Club Ball. On arrival I found that I was the only male person present not in a white tie which posed a problem as to where I should sit. After long consultations in Portuguese, I was led to the "Ambassadors Table." Strangely enough the assembled ambassadors had only two things in common, a total lack of interest in racing and breeding and a very small knowledge of the English language. I contented myself with watching as tremendous a display of jewellery as I have ever seen anywhere, embellishing the necks, breasts and arms of very large ancient ladies and incredibly beautiful young girls.

Because of their association with France, many of the good

83

stallions there were of French breeding including such horses as the Boussac-bred Coaraze.

From Brazil I went to Argentina, whose inhabitants were having a revolution. The road from the airport was lined with tanks all the way to the city, but the revolution seemed to have little effect on the racehorse and stud owners who inhabited the Jockey Club. They almost all talked English and French and many of them had been educated in England or France. They were — and I hope still are — living in great comfort in European style with excellent food and good wine. I did not go to the Bariloche area in the mountains where there is good trout fishing but I did travel about looking at stud farms. The country round Buenos Aires is flat and has excellent grazing facilities. It is also a great place for birds — particularly wading birds — which abound on every little stretch of water.

I visited, of course, the stud farms of the Martinez de Hoz brothers. They had been educated in England at Eton and despite that spoke perfect English! When their father died there had been a dispute about the will and the brothers had never spoken since. The estates were divided by a wire fence. I believe I was one of the first people to visit both of them. They certainly had a marvellous collection of brood mares, nearly all about 15.2 hands — the best height for a brood mare. They had beautiful heads and necks and were usually bays with black points. They all had perfect hocks, because the Argentinians used to race with a curb bit in the horse's mouth and a strong hock was essential. Most of the Martinez de Hoz mares were descendants of Bahram or Rustom Pasha, hence their quality. Chapadmalal and Malhal Hue were model stud farms.

Martinez de Hoz became economics minister after one of the revolutions. He came to England on an exploratory mission and I met him again once or twice. One morning I was rung up by the Foreign Office who asked me if I would take Senor Martinez de Hoz racing at Goodwood. A large limousine appeared and in this we swayed down the country roads of Sussex. The Minister produced a list of fancied horses. Apparently the Foreign Secretary, Lord Home, had rung him up at 8 o'clock that morning and said "I have gone through the card and here are my selections, except for the first race which is an apprentice race and therefore not worth a bet." I am sorry to record that if Martinez de Hoz had backed all the selections he would not have come home a rich man!

The Argentinians have imported some top-class horses and were buying Derby winners in the 19th century. They have been able to produce their own bloodlines and now need only an occasional reintroduction to European or American blood. I sold them among others Snow Cat, bred by the National Stud, who carried the Queen's colours to victory at Ascot in 1958. He was a great success, as was, to a rather lesser extent, Merchant Venturer, second in the 1963 Derby to Relko. I suppose Dancing Moss, found for Pilo Fernandez Guerrico by my partner, Christo Philipson, is the most successful of recent imports.

From Argentina I went to Chile. I contracted "gyppy tummy" in all South American countries but nowhere so badly as in Chile. As essential condition for going to Chile is to have a large supply of brown pills. Apart from that there is some beautiful country. Unfortunately, I could only visit the central part round Valparaiso where there are many stud farms. It is very good country for horse breeding and the horses bred there supply most of the countries in South America with race horses, as well as a number to race in the U.S.A. In almost all the countries I visited there was present a Chilean horse-dealer of some sort, peddling horses. In rather the same way as New Zealand, Chile, having no money to spend, went in for very well-bred potential stallions with little performance — and did well with them.

When I was there, visiting the stud of Senator Amunategui, the leader the Liberal party, I was sitting on the verandah of his house when an earthquake began. It did not last very long and luckily we were outside the house and suffered no damage. I was interested to see that the horses in the nearby paddock took no notice at all of the earthquake and had evidently encountered one before.

It is sad that Chile is now regarded by some Europeans as outside the pale. Not many years after I was there, the communists secured enough votes in a free election to seize the government of the country, though with only a third of the seats in Parliament. They proceeded to play havoc and murdered many of the people whom I had met on my visits. For the only time in history the non-communists rose as one and turned the communists out. They received too little credit for this and are only blamed for the atrocities of the military government which are as nothing to those carried out or threatened by the communists. I do hope this fertile and beautiful country will soon settle down to peace.

Peru was my next port of call. There is a lot to like about the city of Lima, with many traces of Spanish architecture and some attractive gardens. Unfortunately there are factories to the north and south of the city and whichever way the wind blows the industrial smells and smogs sweep over the streets. When I first went there, the oligarchical government, all Spanish in origin, were in full command but various revolutions and near revolutions have turned the government far to the left, and many stud farms and racing stables have been badly affected by the redistribution of land and wealth. It is a difficult place to breed good horses because of the soil and climate but by use of alfalfa and various additivies the job can be done. In the years after the war various well-bred stallions and mares were imported by such well-known breeders as Berckemeyers, the Prados and Ayullo Pardo. There are still good English and French families represented in studs but the whole standard of racing and breeding has fallen owing to the lack of imports.

On one visit to Peru, I came from Saratoga in August. Having only been in Lima previously in their summer (our winter) I had not appreciated that the climate in Lima would be very much colder than in Saratoga. I had no warm clothes with me. On the evening of my arrival I was to be invited to see the English ambassador, one of the few even to try to assist our trade in horses. As it was so comparatively cold, I put on my pyjamas under my tropical suit. All went well until I lifted my glass and displayed a long arm of pyjamas jutting our from my sleeve. I do not think the ambassador thought much of bloodstock agents after that!

Colombia, next door to Peru, is a very different country, as the capital Bogota is high in the mountains, which are the second highest in South America. It makes for a cool climate but some people find the height affects them. The country is run by an oligarchy of Spanish-speaking people of European descent but all around the mountains there are guerilla bands and various collections of rebel activists. When I first went there it was possible — and easy — to go out to the stud farms with none or only a small escort. Now things are more difficult.

Our agent had been educated at an English public school — Stoneyhurst — and retained a perfect command of excellent English. He, Guillermo Aya Villaveces, had the unpromising task of organising the new racecourse and the first race meeting. Apart from anything else all the participants had to be imported from Chile or England. I attended the opening race-meeting and watched in horror as it got darker and darker, so that the last race was run in such bad light that the photo-finish camera would not work, thereby creating a near riot. Racing was a success there for a few years but control fell into the wrong hands and Mr. Ecchevaria bravely arranged the construction of a new course which eventually took over from the first one — and its mafia.

Although the standard of racing was in the first place not high, a good class of breeding horse and mare were imported. One of the most successful was Kessrullah, a good handicapper by Nasrullah, whom we bought from that great gambler Alec Bird. We also imported a class horse from France called San Roman, winner of the Grand Prix de Paris and from England, Red Dragon, the property of the Princess Royal and a good class stayer. The most remarkably successful breeder was Elkin Ecchevaria whose farm was at

Medellin, and whose successful imported stallions included the Lincolnshire Handicap winner Babur and the Holliday horse Trimmer by Nearco.

Another successful stud with high-class mares was owned by Ernesto Puyana, father of the world famous harpsichord player. The Cubillos brothers also had a top-class stud farm, with imported mares and stallions. Owing to the economic situation, imports have become fewer and the standard has (no doubt) dropped. There is also the continual threat of uprising by the Indians, which makes it difficult to visit your own stud. On one of my visits a student protest was in progress and the road from the airport was thick with glass and nails. It took us many detours and three punctures to get to the centre. Bogota is one of those places where it would be pleasant to live if only the guerillas would disappear for ever into the mountains.

I went on to Caracas in Venezuela, a city I visited more than once. It had been hit by the oil boom and enormous unsteady looking skyscrapers had grown up over night, standing next to peasant huts. The peasants sat outside with a machete (knife) in one hand and a pipe in the other, their blankets hanging backwards over their shoulders. Venezuela proudly proclaimed itself a free democracy where elections were held in the European manner. Prosperity was such that a new racecourse had been built in great splendour. The track itself — a dirt track — was a good one, the accommodation comfortable, the totalisator new and the interior of the members' section of the grandstand ostentatious in its decoration.

For years imported horses from England and the USA as well as Argentina and Chile filled the stables. Then the economic situation made the Government restrict importations and lay down the law that Venezuelans must breed and race homebred horses. The standard therefore, declined. You can still import horses of group class in theory but they are too expensive to be worth bringing in.

When I was there one of our clients asked me if I would like to see one of his stud farms near the coast. We went in his own two-engined jet and were met by the farm manager, a man whose large stomach indicated that he was not over-worked. The farm was at sea level with grapefruit trees and palms abounding. There was very little grass and from the condition of the mares I could see that the manager fed himself before the animals. It transpired that the owner had not been there for two years and had no idea of the condition of his horses. I saw red and told both of them how horror-struck I was at seeing mares and foals in that condition. I am glad to say that he shut down the stud, sacked the manager and removed those horses that were not too far gone to another stud further up the mountains.

When being shown round the magnificent new racecourse at Caracas set in a bowl of the hills with the meagre dwellings of the peasants perched all round us, the hosts always repeated the same remark. "One day the natives will come down from the hills and swallow us all up."

Although Mexico is not a part of South America, I think my visits fit better here than as an appendix to the U.S.A. Mexico City is almost as high in the mountains as Bogota and some visitors cannot stand the height. Because of its height a little alcohol goes a long way and the inhabitants drink very little of the "hard stuff". Also because of its height the climate is sunny, but not too hot and almost every afternoon in the rainy season there are a few drops of rain. There are also beautiful gardens and colour to set off the Spanish and French architecture. The main part of the city was designed by the French Emperor Louis Napoleon who was eventually murdered, and wide avenues with trees and shrubs make it a beautiful place to sit in a traffic block.

Although the various Mexican revolutions were supposed to have brought about equalization of wealth and the extermination of the Church, both divisions of wealth between vastly rich and very poor have returned and the church is in operation again. The Mexicans are very proud of their modern architecture, particularly of the building in the University but I myself was more interested in the ancient cathedral, survivor of earthquakes and heathenism, where the peasants still do their penances, crawling on their knees for half a mile up to the great door. The city is full of antique and art shops and a variety of very good restaurants.

A new racecourse was built in the 1940's, on modern lines with great comfort for the spectators. The dirt track is on the heavy side and because of the height a horse needs more stamina than you would expect. If you train a horse in the altitude of Mexico City and then send him down to sea level, say to Florida, in his first one or two races he will do very much better times than in Mexico. After a bit he will revert to his real merit.

The pioneer of Mexican racing was a very wise man called Don Carlos Gomez. He became a friend of Brigadier Scott who found for him some very successful mares and fillies. His best, in fact, was probably Orizaba by Combat, provided by the Anglo-Irish Agency. Although his farm was a dust bowl very near the city, he did his horses well with plenty of alfalfa and they repaid his care. When I was there, he suggested that we visit Acapulco with him to discuss his horses in the relaxed atmosphere of the seaside. Being a Mexican he arrived a day late and so we went swimming on an island connected to the mainland by ferry. There we put all our valuables — such as passport, travellers' cheques, my wallet and some dollars won by my wife at Santa Anita — on a branch of a tree, near the beach so that we could see it as well as the pelicans.

After we bathed during an afternoon of pleasure for the wife and sunburn for me, we set off for the ferry. This was a small rowing boat, full to capacity of returning bathers. As we got off one of the crew "handed" my wife off. One hundred yards up the beach, she suddenly said "Where is my bag?" Although we returned at full speed to the beach, there was no sign of boat or crew. We had therefore lost virtually everything.

The police, of course, found nothing. But they took us to the jail to see if we could identify any of the inmates as our boatman. It was an unforgettable experience to see this collection of human riff-raff collected in one place, all gesticulating rudely or otherwise to ask us for money to bribe the jailers to let them out.

Of course we could not identify our boatman. Don Carlos helped us out and the British Consul issued temporary passports, but nothing was seen of our property. The travellers cheques were never used, nor the credit cards. No dark gentleman used my club identity cards in London but of course, the hard earned winnings in Santa Anita were never seen again.

On one of my visits to Mexico I was dining with some charming people who said "Do you like shooting? If so come and shoot duck with us tomorrow."

At four in the morning I was shown a selection of guns — ten of them Purdeys — to choose from. Cartridges were more of a problem because at that time they were not being made in Mexico City and were hard to import, but by having a whip round they very kindly collected a hundred and fifty or so for me.

We set off in the dark and drove perhaps for an hour and a half. At one point I was told to lie on the floor while we passed some sentries. When we arrived it was still pitch dark, and there was frost on the ground. But they told me that I would need dark glasses when the sun came up — and they were right. A native Indian appeared with a canoe and a double ended paddle. He loaded me and the gun and cartridges into his boat and paddled me out to an island. Before it began to get light, there was absolute silence, but as the first signs of dawn appeared, the air was full of the sound of wings, and soon thousands of duck rose from the lake and flew round.

When it was light, we began shooting. I noticed that my companions did not shoot at the easy ones but waited for the good birds — and seldom missed. I started off in the normal way but soon realized that if I fired at everything in range, I would soon be out of cartridges. My native retriever collected the birds, paddling out at great speed to collect the runners and often coming to blows with the man next door, since they were paid according to the number of duck they

91

brought back. We went on shooting until about 10 o'clock — teal, purple winged teal, mallard, pochard, shovellers, widgeon, canvas backs and what was known as "big duck," a large brown bird not met with in England. I do not know exactly what our bag was but I think it was in the region of four hundred. As soon as we had moved out another team of guns moved in.

Although this was great fun it was not really a very popular activity in North America, where the U.S.A. authorities take great care to limit the numbers of duck shot. These birds were migratory and collected in huge numbers twice a year. The Mexicans took their toll every time they passed through.

Don Carlos Gomez introduced me to a family called Fernandez who owned the racecourse. Don Justo Fernandez was a man of great charm, intelligence and wealth. He was head of the coffee bureau of Central and South America and many other things. Unfortunately he spoke very little English. His wife, who speaks perfect English, is a most intelligent and cultured lady with varied interests and all his numerous sons, who speak English like their wives, share his interest in the English thoroughbred. He has two stud farms outside the city — one at Jalapa and one north of the city, where he has three or four thoroughbred stallions and a collection of mares. It is a very interesting place to visit. The house is square with holes for rifles in various strategic points and a garden and courtyard in the centre. It was once the property of an English lady who eventually made the mistake of being out in her trap during one of the revolutions, becoming a victim of the bandits.

At the farm Mr. Fernandez has not only thoroughbred stallions but Arabs, Apaloosas and Mexican display horses. He has chosen well with English and Irish mares but his American bred stallions have on the whole been more successful than the English, though he had one successful English horse by Grey Sovereign.

The Fernandez horses have the very best of care and comfort and as much good food, including alfalfa, as you can find in a country not usually suited to horse-breeding. They also have "quarter horses" who take part in four furlong races. When the final of the Mexican quarter horse competition takes place between the two qualifiers, huge crowds gather to see the match — and bet on it. Many of the spectators carry arms and the final always ends in bloodshed. Besides quarter horse racing and the track in Mexico City, you can also race at a new track on the borders of the U.S.A. As racing is illegal in Texas, the Mexican track is well attended from over the border.

Anyone going to Mexico and having meals with the inhabitants should be prepared for strange hours and long meals. Lunch is generally at three or four and consists of at least eight courses. Dinner is generally taken about eleven o'clock at night and is anything from eight to twelve courses. Most of them consist of small portions of very hot — highly spiced — food which can have a disastrous effect on a European stomach. With any luck your host or hostess will give guidance about what to avoid. There are in the city extremely good French restaurants, whose owners keep to a European regime.

CHAPTER 8

Australia and New Zealand

AUSTRALIA IS ONE OF the better racing countries of the world. Good class horses race, mainly on turf, at well-conducted race meetings. They are each run by their separate race clubs but under strict discipline. Australia is one of the countries where betting takes place on a very large scale and is well organized. On the course they have bookmakers and the Tote and off course there is only the Tote which has a large number of offices in towns everywhere. The racing authorities get their hands on a fair measure of the proceeds, particularly of the off-course Tote betting. If a bookmaker puts up a price on his board, he is obliged to take it for any amount the punter requires. For instance if he puts up 3-1 and a man comes up and wants 5,000 dollars on at that price the bookmaker has to take it. As the scale of betting is so large, the stewards have to be — and are — very vigilant and very professional. A lot is at stake.

My favourite race meeting in Australia is the carnival meeting in Melbourne. There are, in fact, two such meetings — one in their spring when the Melbourne Cup is run and one in their autumn (i.e. our spring). Owing to the sales times in England I have only seen one Melbourne Cup. This is a two mile handicap on the flat but rather round course. With a big field it takes a bit of riding.

There is a vast amount of betting — ante post and on the day — which is treated as a holiday by most of the inhabitants of that part of Australia. A huge crowd turns up to see what is always a competitive race, won more often than not by a New Zealand bred horse. Many of those in the members and all the men in the Victoria Racing Club stand wear morning coats and top hats. I carried with me the whole regalia throughout a long tour of that part of the world. The fact that my top hat was a black silk one, which was more often to be seen at Ascot or even out with the Heythrop hounds, caused some Australians to reflect on the extraordinary eccentricity of the English.

Beside the Cup, there are a series of weight-for-age races at various distances. The really top-class horses turn out more than once in the week. I saw the great Tulloch run twice in eight days and the actual merit of the best horses in all Australia can be gauged. The Autumn carnival has equally good racing, good handicaps, two-year-old races, everything a connoisseur of racing could want.

In Sydney, some 400 miles north west of Melbourne, the standard of racing is just as high with perhaps more emphasis on two-year-old racing. The Golden Slipper, the championship for two-year-olds, has now a million dollars in added money. The very high stakes all round come from the betting public, although the government take more than their share. On the other hand the Government recognises racing and does a lot for it.

There is argument about where is the best place to breed horses in Australia, but I think that the Hunter Valley north of Sydney can claim to be the most suitable. Although the Hunter River is almost dry in time of drought, there is normally enough water for irrigations, so that alfalfa can be grown. After rains there is a very lush growth of grass, which has to last until it rains again. It is around Scone in the Hunter Valley that many of the large studs are situated. Not far from there is the Widden Valley, always supposed to be the site of the Hidden Valley in Rolf Bolderwood's *Robbery under Arms*, where the Bushrangers "vanished" from the earth with their loot. I have been flown in a small plane over the mountains from which you could see, if you were brave enough to look out, as you twist between the peaks, the one road leading in. If you travel along this road in the evening, you will see numbers of kangaroos and wallabies, coming out of the hills to feed.

At the beginning of the valley was Mr. A.O. Ellison's stud to which Stanley Wootton sent Star King. He had been a top

95

class two-year-old in England in 1948 and trained on up to a point. On arrival in Australia he had to change his name to Star Kingdom and, being only just over 15 hands, he was not immediately hailed as a champion. But when his runners began to appear, it was soon obvious that he was a phenomenal sire. His sons and daughters were unbeatable and unlike any other horse in history, his sons became equally, if not more famous. He revolutionized Australian breeding and why this was so is hard to tell. His sire Stardust, though by Hyperion, has produced nothing else in the same class. But Star Kingdom has left such an impression on Australian breeding, and so many of his sons are at stud that there is almost a danger of in-breeding. A good son or grandson of Star Kingdom in England or Ireland would be of great benefit to our breeding.

Further up the valley at its head is Widden, a beautiful place with a creek and oleanders growing beside it. I have seen it when after rain the creek was so full of water that you could not cross it to the house in a car and the grass has been waist high. But most of the whole area away from the creek itself is as dry as tinder. Oddly enough, horses flourish on what appear to be burned stems of grass eked out by alfalfa. Widden has always been a place where good horses can be bred and Bletchingly (Star Kingdom) has kept up the record.

The owners of Widden were Frank Warwick Thompson and his son Bim, said to be descended from bushrangers. Frank asked me to find him a stallion and when I suggested Edmundo, he and Bim immediately got into an aeroplane and flew over. This was a brave act on his part as he had been almost crippled in a motor accident. We went straight down to see Edmundo, a very nice "quality" horse, not over big and perhaps spoilt by having a light coloured mane and tail. He had been a very good two-year-old in 1955 and just off the top as a sprinter at three. He was by Owen Tudor out of Weighbridge, dam also of Gloria Nicky. Frank looked him over and said "Could we not do better?" So we went the round of the stables and found nothing of which father and son approved. Just before they were due to return, Frank suddenly said " What about that first horse we saw ? " So we leapt into the car and had another look at Edmundo. This time he passed him. It was just as well he did because he was a great success, almost always high up on the stallions' list in Australia. Sadly Frank died and Bim was killed but the stud continues as a successful company.

One of the more beautiful places in New South Wales where horses are bred is the Kellys' Newhaven Park Stud, near Boorowa, within easy motoring distance of both Sydney and Canberra. There the gum trees are at their best and good land breeds good horses. The Kellys have had many good horses but none better than Wilkes by Court Martial ex Sans Pares who was purchased through the BBA for a comparatively small sum. He has left at least one good son called Vain at stud in Australia.

Although Victoria has a more temperate climate, colder winters and more rain, the land is hardly better for breeding horses. The leading stud there was started by the late E.A. Underwood, who stood among other horses, the National Stud bred Landau, who raced in the Queen's colours in England in 1953 and 1954. He did well as a sire in Australia.

When Mr. Underwood died, Mr. Kenneth Cox took the stud over and has had great success ever since. His best horse was Showdown, which the BBA bought for him. He won the Coventry and the Middle Park in 1963 when trained by Fred Winter Senior in Kent, and was just off the top at three, fourth in the 2000 Guineas being about his measure. He was by Infatuation, a Nearco horse who bred little else of note before vanishing to Japan, out of the great mare Zanzara. He has certainly left his mark in Australia both as a sire and sire of broodmares.

South Australia is that much hotter and drier than Victoria yet they are able to breed horses successfully. One of the show places there is Lindsay Park near Angaston, north east of Adelaide, belonging to Colin Hayes, an ex-amateur rider and absolutely top trainer. You drive through the Barossa Valley, where much of the best wine in Australia is grown and made, and on to Lindsay Park where the Hayes have

97

made a beautiful garden. There are also English-style grass gallops and stabling for perhaps a hundred racehorses. Three or four stallions stand there always. Among the more successful horses were Romantic from the Pretty Polly family, a good sire of two-year-olds and Estaminet who, though hard to deal with, has done well. But Without Fear, whom I sold Colin in five minutes over the telephone, has had an unbeatable record largely in two-year-old races. He ran in France and England in the colours of Mr. Howell Jackson.

To go to Lindsay Park on a hot day and find the top class rider Ron Hutchinson lying in the swimming pool and the (tame) deer watching him through the fence is an experience in itself. Colin, although he has had operations for his heart, leads an energetic life, often working his horses first lot in Adelaide, then flying to Melbourne to see his team work there. Nowadays he stands some of Robert Sangster's more successful horses.

In Queensland, where they run the big winter races, there is a belt of red earth which is a good place to breed horses. But there has never been quite the money behind Queensland breeders as in New South Wales. I was once asked to find a moderate priced stallion for the Krugers at their Lyndhurst Stud near Warwick, south west of Brisbane, and recommended to them a handicapper called Grand Chaudiere, which they bought for a reasonable price. He has been a success there since he was by a horse called Northern Dancer, whose fame was not so widely recognised then as it is today.

Western Australia is a very long way across the desert — 2,500 miles in round figures from Brisbane to Perth and a whole night's flight from Adelaide. Racing and breeding there is very much improved as the prosperity of the state has increased. They now run some very valuable races there for which the rest of Australia has to compete. Now that horses can be so easily flown across the desert the travel problem is not insurmountable.

I got myself in trouble in Perth one day when attending the races. There was a two-year-old sweepstake for horses bred by their owners in Western Australia with a very big prize attached. Australians are great people for long speeches and it is the custom for words to be spoken over the microphone to the crowd after the race is over. I was asked to congratulate the owner/breeder of the winner. I started off alright, but, when I got to congratulating the breeder there were hoots and roars. I thought it was their way of greeting an English accent. But in fact, unknown to me, there was controversy as to whether the owner had, in fact, bred the horse. The case went to the stewards and dragged on into threats and law suits. I think the result stood.

On another occasion I was asked to address the Victorian breeders in Melbourne. I drew up a long carefully thought out speech, which I hopefully believed was witty. I was somewhat put off by the silence with which even the jokes were greeted. It was only when I sat down that someone at the back said, "You know the microphone was never switched on and we only saw your lips moving!"

Australia is not all racing. When I first went there a dinner was given for me at the Melbourne Club at which all the drinks were to be Australian. We started off with dry sherry, very good too. Then there was an excellent white wine and some good red wine. I had great difficulty in getting down the port and found the brandy, though very drinkable, strong enough to produce a fearful hangover. The two areas where the best wine is made are the Hunter Valley, where so many good studs are situated and the Barossa Valley in South Australia, close to Colin Hayes's stud. The standard of Australian wines is extremely good, particularly the white — and bears no relation to bulk export of "plonk," mostly from Western Australia, which is sold cheaply in Europe. They would not be tolerated in Australia. Very little of the good wine is allowed out of the country. How wise!

The BBA's business in Australia was, and is, arranged through agents of whom three were picked out by Brigadier Scott and gave us outstanding service. In New South Wales John Inglis, a huge powerful man, who could auction

99

yearlings for three days on end and then sell several hundred head of cattle, is our man. He has only one fault. Never stand near him if he is watching a race in which he has had a bet — or you are in danger of having a heavy handfall, like a sledge-hammer, on your shoulder as he shouts his fancy home! In Victoria we have been helped over the years by Bill Stutt, as good a judge of a horse as you will find anywhere, and in South Australia by David Coles, a great auctioneer and go-getter, who now looks after Robert Sangster's interests in the Antipodes.

One of the features of the great cities of Australia are the clubs, where if you are "put up" and sponsored by a member you can stay in Victorian comfort. The Melbourne Club, most of whose members are graziers from the Western District — the aristocracy of Australia — is a very good place to stay. On my first visit I was woken at 6.30, the usual time in Australia, by a man who saluted and offered me a cup of tea.

"Were you at Vimy or Messines or Gallipoli, sir?" he said.

I was clearly a disappointment to him when I had to admit that I had not been born by then. Women, who are just getting emancipated in Australia, were, of course, only allowed in the club at certain times and on social occasions.

In Adelaide, where the club was equally comfortable, I got myself in trouble. I had been out to dinner with a doctor who was head of the breeders association in South Australia. When we got back to the club, I asked him in for a drink. Just as we were settled down over a whisky and soda, the hall porter appeared and said "Sir, your guest is not a member and as a temporary member you are not allowed to ask a non-member in. He must leave!" And leave he did, without his whisky.

There is considerable competition to become members of these clubs and blackballing is more common than in England. But their existence was a great boon to visiting Englishmen particularly if they were affiliated to their London club.

One day while at the races, I was talking to Sir Chester Manifold. "Chetty" Manifold had been a great innovator in Victorian racing and had pioneered — at some danger to himself — the introduction of Tote betting off-course. He lived in the Western District. He told me that he had a good steeplechaser, the best in Australia. He had won everything of any class and now was hard to place. He had been invited to race in an international race in the U.S.A. He wondered if it was worth sending him to England to try his luck there. I looked up his form and found it to be good. He was a big strong jumping type of horse. So I suggested that he should be sent on from the U.S.A. to England. "All right," he said, "find me a trainer." I thought for a bit and came up with the name of Fred Winter. Sir Chester agreed, and so, when I went home, I arranged for Fred to train him. The horse was Crisp and there is no need to remind readers of his remarkable race in the 1973 Grand National, giving away nearly two stone to the triple National winner Red Rum, jumping brilliantly and only being caught close home. Sir Chester came over to see him run in the 1972 Cheltenham Gold Cup where he ran with credit, but he could not get away for the National.

When the time came to retire Crisp, Fred Winter arranged for him to go to Colonel John Trotter in Yorkshire. At first he was a fearsome ride — bucking, kicking, shying, rearing. One day when riding him on the farm the Colonel saw a sheep on its back caught up in wire. The only thing to do was to leap off Crisp, throw the reins over his head and go to the rescue of the sheep — risking a long walk home. But the old horse stood still as a rock, remembering his early days in Australia, rounding up sheep and forever after that he was a reasonable and sensible ride. He became a hunter and the Colonel rode him in front as Field Master; but there was a strict rule that he never stayed out after one o'clock. So a great horse had a happy retirement. Would it have been too much for the Gods to have robbed Red Rum of one of his Nationals and allowed this gallant traveller from Victoria to have kept his head in front?

101

NEW ZEALAND

New Zealand is a very different country from Australia. It is two and a half hours by air from either Melbourne or Sydney to Auckland and the climate and scenery on arrival is very different. Whereas in Australia breeding horses is a constant struggle against the lack of rain, New Zealand has almost perfect conditions — plenty of good grass, limestone, pure water, land which has not yet been overdone with horses and additives. The climate is such that you can foal out of doors and for most of the year hardly any additional feeding is required. As a result New Zealand has something in common with Ireland in providing good horses for export. Because they did not have the resources from an economy based on sheep to buy expensive well-performed stallions, the New Zealanders had to learn the English stud book by heart. They knew that they could not buy well performed horses but they could be very strict on conformation and pedigree. To discuss pedigrees with the average New Zealand farmer, you need a great deal more knowledge than you would believe.

The main market for New Zealand horses is Australia and as Australia bred so many fast horses, New Zealanders concentrated for years on more stamina. At the main yearling sales, nearly all the top priced lots go to Australia, though nowadays Americans and Japanese join in. Prices have now reached international level and the production of yearlings is becoming more and more professional.

The economic life of a New Zealand farmer is very often in the hands of a firm of agents such as Wrightsons, who lend him some money to help him buy his farm and his sheep, finance his seed buying, his stallion purchases and finally sell the end product for him. Wrightsons have been the agents of the BBA for fifty years or so — and very good ones at that.

When buying a stallion for a New Zealand breeder — or, for that matter breeders from South Africa or Australia, you are taking on a very serious commitment. It is usual for the owner of, say, 100 mares to have one, two or three stallions. When he gets a new horse at least 30, possibly 50, of his mares go to that horse. The next year he sees their foals on the ground, all in one place. He gets an immediate idea of their quality. Imagine in England, Ireland or France trying to see the first crop of your stallion who are spread out all over the place. Your new stallion's crop grow into yearlings and what you think of them is unimportant compared to what the public are prepared to pay at auctions. You are desperate for a good sale. Then comes the racecourse test. If the two-year-olds do not win, you are left with at least another three crops on the way which no-one will want to buy. The agent who is buying a stallion, must therefore have in mind the great responsibility which rests on his shoulders.

Even the best studs in New Zealand need a good stallion to keep them in business. Seton Otway's famous Trelawney Stud, near Cambridge and some 70 miles south of Auckland went right to the top and stayed there with Balloch, Foxbridge and Alcimedes. Balloch had never run and Seton Otway tried to repeat the experiment by coming over himself to buy two yearlings which he intended not to race but to use as stallions. This experiment did not work and the stud went through, for them, a lean period until their new horse Wolverton (1976) began to show how good a sire he was, Wolverton being a son of the 1969 Eclipse Stakes winner Wolver Hollow.

On the other hand, one day in 1963 I heard that a two-year-old colt by Never Say Die, out of the great Meld, who had been in Sir Cecil Boyd-Rochfort's stable at Newmarket, had split a pastern and was for sale. I had a long look at him at the stud of his owner-breeders, Sir Harold and Lady Zia Wernher, on behalf of Brian Anderton, a client in the South Island of New Zealand, whom Wrightsons persuaded to buy. The colt was called Mellay, who became the leading sire in New Zealand. He was a half brother to Lady Zia Wernher's 1967 Derby winner Charlottown.

The list of good stallions sent to New Zealand by the BBA is too long to reproduce in detail but a few, not necessarily the best, are worth alluding to. When we were offered in 1949 Faux Tirage, an unbeaten own brother of Combat, there was apparently a hurry so we cabled him first to New Zealand for Tom Lowry (T.C. Lowry of cricket fame) of the Okawa Stud, Hastings, and a little later to Australia for John Kelly of the Newhaven Park Stud in New South Wales. Of course both accepted him the same day. So we gave the verdict to the one whose cable had the earlier time. By King George V's 1942 2000 Guineas winner Big Game out of the 1941 Oaks winner Commotion he was superbly bred and very successful.

So was Oncidium, whose temperament on the racecourse rather let him down in England. Owned and bred by Lord Howard de Walden, he was the winner of the 1965 Coronation Cup. If you have to give way in some respect in order to get a horse for your price, I think ungenuineness is an acceptable fault. The reason may be physical and something which we cannot detect. Rego, for instance, bought for Carl Powell in New South Wales for 1,100 guineas was an example of a Nasrullah who won all the gallops and few races. He was a great success.

New Zealanders are prepared to accept French horses or those who race there and Zamazaan has repaid their faith in very well-bred staying horses. Sir Tristram, belonging to Patrick Hogan of the Cambridge Stud is a rather different case. The family had done well with such horses as Blueskin and Final Call which I had found for them. But as New Zealand sales prices move up in the world, they wanted something better. Patrick picked out the Sir Ivor horse, Sir Tristram, in France, and asked Sir Philip Payne-Gallwey to go over and see him. He sent a glowing report on most of the horse but remarked that he had very bad hocks. Either Patrick did not read to the end of the cable or he took the risk and bought him. He confessed to a state of shock when he saw him on arrival but now that he is the outstanding sire in New Zealand — and Australia — I think he overlooks the hocks! Oddly enough Delville Wood (by Bois Roussel), a very successful sire in New South Wales, was turned down by my partners on account of his hocks. In England at the moment Sharpo seems to be surviving any snide remarks about his hocks and in no uncertain manner. But don't try to sell those with bent hocks to an Argentinian.

One of the facts of life for a stallion in New Zealand is that there is hardly any limit to the number of mares he is asked to cover. A moderate racehorse called Alvaro, whom I sold to a farm in the Waikato area in the North Island, did so well that when I visited him he had just covered his 100th mare that season!

There are now almost too many farmers breeding horses in New Zealand and the tendency now is more for syndicates to acquire top class horses for large sums than to buy the well-bred second class racehorse. These horses are, of course, harder to find than such as Sovereign Edition whom we bought for Sir Woolf Fisher of the Ra Ora Stud and who carried Grey Sovereign's influence to the very top in the Antipodes.

No-one who spends any time in New Zealand should fail to have a day or two trout fishing. I remember the scene at Lake Taupo in the centre of the North Island when dozens of fishermen were converging on the points where streams went into the lake. The game was to cast further out than anyone and trawl a wet fly back towards you. With a long line out you had to be very accurate not to catch your nearest neighbour in the ear — a crime in New Zealand equivalent to shooting your host's keeper over here!

New Zealand, of course, has a good trade in jumpers and can breed a tough type of all purpose horse rather in the same brand as Irish bred steeplechasers. But it is a long way to bring them home. Nevertheless, it would be a great mistake to underrate the quality of New Zealand horses or the charm of the countryside.

CHAPTER 9

South Africa, Italy and Sweden

THERE ARE MANY other parts of the world, including Japan and the West Indian islands where I made visits on horse business. But I think it best to let off anyone who has got as far as this with a short account of South Africa.

It is difficult to mention the word South Africa without visions of political repression and misery on all sides. This is, of course, not a true picture and you can travel most of the country without any idea of the turmoil in the black quarters round the big cities which certain journalists seem to thrive on.

For climate and beauty there are few places to beat South Africa. The horses are bred either on the dry limestone of the Karoo, a high level plain with more limestone than water, or in the lush areas of the Western Cape. The Karoo plain, (between Johannesburg and Cape Town) used to be far in front but with the death of some of the big farm owners there, the Western Cape has probably taken the lead.

Racing is excellently run in the main centres in South Africa. There is a great deal of betting, particularly ante-post on the big races such as the July Handicap at Durban. So much so that on one occasion a man fired a bullet into the quarters of the ante-post favourite while he was at exercise. The horse recovered and the bookmaker lost his money! Racing is comfortable for both black and white as Lord Wyatt, Chairman of the Horserace Totalisator Board, pointed out in his articles on his return from a recent visit.

One of the most remarkable places to visit is the stud farms owned by the Birch Brothers in the wilds of Cape Province, some 60 miles from Dordrecht. The studs are now owned not by brothers but by first cousins. They always consign fifty or more yearlings to the sales and, until very recently, were the leading sellers and leading breeders. "Bot" Birch, the eldest cousin, is president of the breeders' association and has done a great deal for South African breeding.

When one arrives at Dordrecht one is immediately reminded of the Highlands of Scotland. Low hills, rocks and, if there has been rain, lakes or lochs only lack the heather to complete the illusion. There they keep five or six stallions and two or three hundred mares, as well as a thriving native population. As they say, they breed their own grooms.

One day when I arrived there, a tall black figure rose from among the beds of red cannas in front of the house and let out a flow of language. I thought at least that he was announcing the arrival of the Boers but my host told me that he said: "Boss, here is the man who comes to sell you horses." Pretty good observation from a gardener. I asked him to reply "I hope so."

Once when I was staying with the Birches, I was taken along to attend the wedding of a boy and girl, one of whom was a Boer and one of British descent. This was the first event of that sort in the area in living memory and outlined to me the sad fact that the Boer war has never ended.

As in all such studs the success or otherwise depends on having a good stallion or two. The Birches' success after the war was founded on the exploits of Fairthorn, a Fair Trial horse bought for them by Brigadier Scott. The Sandringham-bred High Veldt, bought through Keith Freeman, was only a small horse but, like his sire Hyperion, capable of breeding sturdy yearlings and good racehorses. But the Birches really hit the jackpot with Plum Bold (Bold Ruler ex Plum Cake). Philip Payne-Gallwey and I between us located him in America and brought him out of the country. Sadly for the Birches he did so well that the almighty dollar bought him back. Several other American-breds were not so successful for the Birches, though the Scott brothers stand an American bred horse, Jungle Cove (USA), who was top of the sires list in 1986.

The BBA has as their agent in the Southern Cape, Sir Mordaunt Milner, a successful breeder and author, whose

107

stud is at his home at Klapmuts, some thirty miles north of Cape Town. He did remarkably well with stallions and fillies bought for comparatively small sums, including St. Cuthbert, tracing to Pretty Polly and bought for 5,000 guineas at an Ascot sale. The system he used was to pick out on pedigree some sale offerings which would appeal to South Africa and to get me to look at them. Some of his selections were, to say the least, strange, but when you looked into the pedigree you found what had been for him its attraction. The severe restrictions on imports set by the South African breeders to limit competition from overseas has made his kind of buying more difficult. But a good man with a catalogue can find all sorts of things.

Racehorses, mainly in the form of fillies, have been very successful when imported, provided they have speed, since the emphasis is on short distance races. Among these who have excelled are Sparkling Susie, Duchess of Sussex (bought as a yearling), En Avant and Lady of Habit. South Africans also like to import horses as stallions and race them first. This method sometimes allows a loophole in the import restrictions. Horses such as On Stage have raced very successfully before going to stud. But naturally it does not always work.

One of the most successful studs in South Africa is Highlands, situated in the Southern Cape. It now belongs to Mr. Graham Beck. When it was owned by the late Jack Stubbs, a past Chairman of the Cape Turf Club, he asked me to find him a stallion. When I got home and looked round a bit, I found that a horse called Persian Wonder by Persian Gulf, owned and bred by Lord Durham and trained in his first two seasons by Jack Colling, was for sale. He had won five races off the reel as a two-year-old and the Dee Stakes at Chester as a three-year-old but the handicapper had then got his measure and he usually found one too good for him.

Persian Wonder was a very attractive individual with a lovely head and neck and a large bold eye. He had his faults in other directions and was a long horse, though not very tall. He came of the same female line as the flying Mumtaz Mahal and Lady Juror, his second dam being a very fast mare called Belle Travers.

I got in touch with Jack Stubbs and suggested he should buy him for the large sum of 7,000 guineas. His immediate reaction was to ring up Sir Jack Jarvis, who made several visits in the winter to the Cape. Jack Jarvis said that he would investigate and got on the telephone to Jack Colling. The conversation, I understand, went like this.

"Jack, you used to train a horse called Persian Wonder. I understand his owner wants to sell him?"

"Yes, he has won nine and he has got too high in the handicap."

"Would he do for a friend of mine in South Africa?"

"Yes, he would make a stallion all right."

Jack Jarvis picked up the other telephone, rang Jack Stubbs and said that he should buy Persian Wonder. He did not even go to see him. But Jack took the word of the great man, who had not even given him a description of the horse.

Jack Stubbs ignored my advice not to race the horse. He said he would put him in training and instruct his trainer only to run him if he was going to win. Unfortunately he did run him a few times and he ran very badly, so that when he went to stud he had shown himself apparently inferior to several South African horses. Consequently he did not attract much patronage from outside breeders.

Fortunately Jack Stubbs had a very good stud manager in Colin Tyler and a good broodmare band, many of them bought by us in England, so that when I came out two years or so later, the first yearlings by Persian Wonder were being prepared for the sales. I fell in love with them immediately. They were all of the same type, dark brown, good head, neck and eye, all quality, not very big. He had certainly stamped his stock. I went through South Africa, saying to anyone interested that they were the best first crop in the country.

They sold fairly well at the yearling sales. But when they began to run as two-year-olds, they really took off. In no time Persian Wonder was the leading sire and as many of his earlier successes were through horses out of English

109

imported mares, I felt he was a horse to be proud of. Later on after heading the sires list several times his mares were to prove equally effective.

What was the reason for his phenomenal success is hard to discover. He was admittedly by a good sire of sires but there were no sires close up in his female line — just a very good racing family. Mordaunt Milner was one of the earliest to appreciate how good he was destined to be and profited accordingly.

At one December Sales, we were buying for Highlands and picked out a mare by Court Martial called No Ball in foal to Sovereign Path. We bought her and sent a cable to the Stubbs to say "Have bought you No Ball. Don't worry this is not a stallion!" She foaled a colt by Sovereign Path who was called rather appropriately, Lords. He was a good sprinter and in due course a very successful stallion.

South Africa is such a pleasant place, climatically and scenically, that I hope it survives its present troubles. It has everything in the world in resources except for oil and, given luck and a free hand to conduct its own affairs, could be a great power in the world, despite the continuing war between the Boers and the later invaders.

ITALY

Italy is a long way from South Africa but has in some ways a similar climate. Although it is not a natural horse-breeding country, it has attained fame in the bloodstock world mainly through the genius of Signor Federico Tesio. By the time I came along, he was dead but I got to know his widow Donna Lydia very well. She was a remarkable woman, fluent in eight languages and with a wide knowledge of all sorts of cultural subjects besides racehorses. Her principal residence was at Dormello, north-east of Milan, in a house built by Signor Tesio, who was an architect. One of the features of this place was a summer house, which was so sited that even on the hottest day it attracted a breeze from across Lake Maggiore.

Although so many great horses were bred at Dormello, it was hardly what you call good horse country. Many of the paddocks were undulating and rock strewn, without much summer grass. Signor Tesio had used the services of the BBA through Brigadier Scott for many years and among the horses we had brought from him were Donatello II and Nearco. Tesio was always short of funds and partly to remedy this he took as his partner Marchese Mario Inchesa della Rochetta, who lived mainly in Switzerland. With his help they developed a stud at Olgiata near Rome where the yearlings could be kept during the winter, spring and summer. Mario Inchesa was a man of great intelligence but he presided over a period when the fortunes of the stud went downward. He tried to revive it in the 1970's by buying mares of good pedigree and no performance, turning a blind eye to the faults of their conformation. But this did not really work.

We used to stay with Donna Lydia at Dormello and in Rome at Oligiata with Mario Inchesa. One day returning from the races, Mario, who had looked after us so well, but in a formal manner as if it was a duty, suddenly stopped the car outside one of the great churches of Rome. He then took us on a tour of the principal masterpieces, knowing exactly where to go in each church to find what was best. By the time he had finished and we sat down to dinner, he was not only a client, but a friend.

The Dormello – Oligata stud suffered a further blow when his son-in-law, Count Hunyadi, died young and his elder son came to England. But the stud still produces fancied candidates for all the big Italian races and, of course, its bloodlines have a predominant influence all over the world.

SWEDEN

I also used to visit Sweden annually for the Swedish Derby, held at Malmo in the south west corner of the country. It is surprising that a country so far to the north and so far persuaded of the virtues of Socialism should have had a

National Stud. But until recently they did have this National Stud and the BBA provided the stallions, of whom the Hyperion horse Hyperbole, bought in 1954 at the J.V. Rank dispersal sale and the Loder-bred Carnoustie were probably the best.

Not so far from the National Stud at Vasaholm, Mr. Gosta Dalman had a stud, which passed to the Wettermarks. They were lucky enough to buy the Astor-bred Hornbeam, second in the 1956 St Leger, a private deal, which I arranged, before his virtues were apparent in England. Hornbeam, who was by Hyperion, was remarkably successful in Sweden and was succeeded in 1969 by the miler Jimmy Reppin who almost always headed the list, until his death, with a very high percentage of winners.

The country round Malmo is attractive to look at but the soil is sandy and does not make the breeding of horses easy. But for the Derby there were always tremendous parties in the various castles still lived in by those of the aristocracy, who had survived the Socialist regime in the country. These used to go on all night and end up with a drive to Falsterbo on the Baltic to bathe in the sea at dawn. The hosts would pool their servants so that you would see the same butler at two different castles on successive nights. For the occasional visit one of the difficulties was to catch up with who had re-married whom since last summer and consequently who was your host and hostess in which castle!

One of my friends in Sweden was Carl Bretel Nathhorst. He had been a successful businessman and had at first invested his riches in modern paintings of which he had a remarkable collection. He had a daughter who was interested in horses and she persuaded him to buy a few yearlings, which he did through Scottie and myself. In the short time that he had horses in training he had success. One of the best horses was Lucky Finish, who won the 1968 Dante Stakes at York. Jack Leader trained him and thought he would win the Irish Derby. As he had the good filly Never Red at the same time, they both went over to the Curragh to be ridden by Brian Taylor in the Irish Derby and Pretty Polly

Stakes. The Nathhorsts came over and saw Lucky Finish, unsuited by the firm going, finish a close-up fifth in the Irish Derby behind Ribero.

The filly ran even better and after a bumping finish was placed second. Brian Taylor jumped off, saying that if he objected he was sure to get the race. So in he went to "lodge a fiver." When he was already in the stewards' room the Nathhorsts came up, having been delayed in the crowd. I explained what was happening and was horrified when "Pompe" as he was known, threw up his hands and said "I never object. I would not accept a victory on an objection." While I was wondering how such an attitude fitted in with the Rules of Racing, we heard that the stewards had over-ruled the objection but returned Brian Taylor's deposit.

Although the Nathhorsts had success, they soon moved to California and spent most of their time there or in the South of France, so their racing activities in England came to an end.

In the woods not far from the Wettermarks, there was a large stud farm owned by a man who had trading interests in Pakistan and East Africa. When he died he left his farm and stock to one of his grandchildren, Miss Kirsten Rausing, who became so enthusiastic about racing and breeding that she came over to England and bought the Lanwades Stud from Colonel Nat Frieze, where she now stands the Nijinsky horse Niniski.

CHAPTER 10

Syndications

SELLING AND BUYING HORSES was not the only business activity of mine during my years with the BBA. One of the new adventures which I helped to start was the syndication of stallions and the sale of nominations. Twenty five years ago most stallions were privately owned and you applied to the stud for a nomination at the advertised fee, perhaps £300-£400 for a top horse. This gave even a classic winner a low enough paper value to attract foreigners who wanted to buy.

The almighty dollar enabled the Americans to buy a whole series of our top horses. Partly in order to combat this, English breeders began to form syndicates for our horses at stud. This added enormously to the paper value of stallions. A horse syndicated at £2,000 a share became worth £80,000 immediately. At first there were few horses who were syndicated. Two of the exceptions were Nearco and Prince Chevalier. However the idea soon spread and almost anything that won a good race, even a handicap, was liable to be offered for syndication.

The BBA employed Douglas Hamilton, who had been in the stud world since he was a boy, first at Lord Carnarvon's stud at Highclere in Hampshire. He had spent some years at Burton Agnes in Yorkshire with Marcus Wickham-Boynton and knew the ins and outs of breeding ways. With my encouragement he set up a stallion department at the BBA dealing with syndication and subsequently secretarial work for syndicates. One of the difficulties of syndication was that each share owner could ask what he thought fit for his nomination, so that someone wanting to use a certain horse might have to ring round to thirty share owners to find a suitable nomination at a fair price.

Douglas Hamilton set up the first stallion stock market, as

it were. You rang him and asked for a specific nomination or a recommendation and he would set about obtaining it. Unfortunately stallion owners and committees often over-priced their nominations, as there was no open market to judge by. For that reason Tattersalls and ourselves ran joint auctions of stallion shares and nominations. These, too, posed a danger to stallion owners, because one outrageously high price, as sometimes happens at auction, set a ridiculous standard for a horse, whereas some horse, who was not popular, might lose its value altogether if some nominations sold at very low prices. Syndicates soon got wise to this and many of them put in the agreement that nominations were not to be sold at auction. This really put an end to the Tattersalls/BBA auctions, though Doncaster Sales hold their own sales of share and nominations — a useful service.

Now the BBA circulate lists of horses and their prices and I think provide at least a guide to breeders. Some syndicates fill immediately and some do not. Some escalate in value and some fizzle out altogether. But my own strangest experience was when we were asked by the then trainer Peter Nelson to syndicate a horse belonging to Sir Charles Clore. A few days after advertising it, I was sent for by Sir Charles.

"What do you mean by syndicating my horse?" he said.

"We have done it on the instructions of your trainer, who has your authority to act."

"It was not my instruction and you have got it far too low. He is worth much more."

"I am afraid your trainer did give us the instructions but as to price, you need not worry. On the present offer there has been only one buyer and so the syndicate can be said to have failed."

Sir Charles had a good grumble and kept the horse in training but who was right and who was wrong about his value will never be known because the horse died within nine months.

It is generally considered by those who do not know, that the world of horse-trading is mainly composed of thieves. Horse-dealers are considered in general as crooks and

115

bloodstock agents as not much better. My experience does not bear out this idea. Very large sums of money change hands by nod of head or word of mouth. The auction companies have strict rules about unsoundness for which horses can be returned. Any sensible agent only sells when there is confirmation of soundness by an independent vet. It is very, very seldom that clients — or agents — go back on their word whether it is by telephone or in person.

When it comes to paying for a purchase, that is a different matter. Bad debts of the BBA were virtually non-existent until the 1972/3 economic crisis. From then on they have never ceased to increase. There is the man who when he buys has no intention of paying. There is the overseas client who cannot get the money out of his country because of government restrictions. And there is the man who always puts off payment as long as he can get away with it.

The BBA pay out on the receipt of a veterinary certificate or the bill from the sellers. But you can still be involved in argument over what is sound and what is not. No vet is infallible; horses cannot tell you of their secret ailments. The most awkward dilemma for an agent is whether to send a horse abroad before it has been paid for. Sometimes, if it has been sold C.I.F. (i.e. at a price on delivery including freight and insurance), you cannot draw the money until the horse has arrived. A small error in filling in the papers can delay settlement for months.

While the majority of clients pay up and keep to their word, it cannot be said that all sellers are straight along the line. One great, now deceased, trainer in France always put the price up just as the deal appeared to be completed. It has been known for an otherwise respectable English owner to renege on a verbal option, leaving the foreign buyer with a distorted view of English honesty.

All the years I was with the BBA, I was only involved in two law suits — both times, let me say at once, as a witness — not myself in the dock! The first case concerned a filly, called Mummy's Darling bought to go to South Africa. She had won a few races and my client wanted her to race. The deal was arranged with the trainer, Richard Hannon, who owned a half share in the filly and the vet passed her sound. At that point the owner of the other half said he wanted to run her in one more race. My client found this very inconvenient but agreed on two conditions, that he had half the stakes if she won and that she had another veterinary examination after the race.

She duly won, whereupon the part owner said that he would not sell. My client said that he wanted to sue for possession. To my surprise the owner would not give way and the case went to law. Before the case, the filly was examined by the vet who did not pass her as sound. The deal fell through. But my client instructed us to sue for half the stakes as had been arranged before she ran, so there was a large case for a small amount.

I had never attended a court case before and was astounded at the numbers of men in wigs, all no doubt drawing fees, who were on duty. I had three or more hours in the witness box, while short snap answers were written down in long hand — and then I left for America. After I had gone, the owner put up such a performance in the witness box that the judge told him to leave it. We won the case plus the considerable costs. I am told that what turned the case in our favour was an answer by Richard Hannon to a question as to why he decided to stand by the sale. He said "Because I did not want to let down the Colonel. I was not going to go back on my word." That impressed the judge.

The other case was the famous one when Tattersalls were sued over the sale of a yearling. I was called in as an independent witness as to what was the usual practice at bloodstock sales. I thought this would take ten minutes. Not so. I was four and a half hours being interrogated by two hostile and one friendly lawyer. I was most impressed by the judge's quickness at grasping points in a field of which he was generally ignorant. I was asked, for instance by counsel, "Do you know how Mr. Robert Sangster indicates to the auctioneer that he wants to bid?" I had just time to say "No, I do not and if I did I could not tell you," when the judge jumped in and said "You need not answer that question. It is a matter of confidentiality."

I was most impressed in both cases by the speed with which both judges picked up the points, some of which were obscure to anyone who did not know much about racing. One of them I understood had been given the job twenty-four hours before the case, as the original judge was involved in a European hearing at the European Economic Community. I also learnt that the more oily the lawyer who was questioning you, the more certain it was that he was trying to catch you out.

Apart from a few horse deals I did also make one arrangement for the BBA which was eminently satisfactory for all concerned. As I had remained in the army for several years after the war, I was a long way behind by 1953/4 when I first went to America. Already the most likely clients had been acquired by Frankie More O'Ferrall, David McCall, Keith Freeman, Peter Wragg and the firm of Tim Vigors and Co. One of the Vigors representatives in the U.S.A. was Tom Cooper whom I kept meeting in America, already with his feet under many of the better tables. He seemed to have secured various clients who would otherwise have come to me. Furthermore, he was extremely well-spoken of by everyone in America who knew him. He and Noel O'Callaghan had helped Tim Vigors to build up a thriving business, particularly in the States. Just when things were going well for them, Tim Vigors decided, for reasons unconnected with horses, to move out of Ireland. That seemed to leave the rest of his firm rather high and dry. Tom Cooper, I am glad to say, came to me and asked if we would be interested in buying T. Vigors and Co. The price for the whole firm would not now buy one decent yearling.

Nevertheless I had the greatest difficulty in persuading the partners to come to an arrangement by which we took over that firm and changed its name to BBA (Ireland). That in itself caused a little bit of difficulty, because there were only a few Irishmen literate enough to translate B.B.A. into British Bloodstock Agency! But by careful use of the initials

118

only, Tom Cooper and Noel O'Callaghan kept afloat and built up a very good business indeed. They traded independently of us except in financial matters and, if they did clash with us, it would be at one of the big sales, where their clients might outbid ours or vice versa. But while we tried not to "take each other on" too often, it did not make much difference as clients can and do bid what they like and through whom they like.

After years of successful trading the BBA (Ireland) was closely integrated when the BBA went public in 1984 and I hope the happy and successful relationship will continue for a long time. Tom's eye for a horse and patient technique with clients enabled him to buy a number of Derby and National winners in rapid succession — a process which I hope has not come to an end.

The only serious disagreement with Tom which I have had personally was when he met me at Dublin Airport and said "We are going to take a short cut to The Curragh." After threading our way through little lanes and various encampments of tinkers, Tom, who knew Ireland like the back of his hand, came to a halt in a peat bog with no way forward and a web of twisty lanes behind. So we missed the first race and a damn good lunch with the Turf Club!

CHAPTER 11

Dispersal Sales

I SUPPOSE IT WAS THE 1964 National Stud dispersal sale which accelerated the flow of really top-class mares to America, in which I am afraid I took part. At this dispersal sale the National Stud's mares and young stock were all sold, and I had a strong hand and bought four or five of the highest priced lots. One was the 1957 Oaks winner Caretta, whom I bought for Mrs. Augustus, whom I have already mentioned as aunt of Danny Van Clief. She gave me 50,000 guineas to buy the mare and as we got Caretta for only 20,000 guineas, she expressed surprise. No American agent she had used had ever bought anything for her at *less* than her bid. Sadly the foal by St. Paddy, which she was carrying, was born with a heart defect and she soon tired of the mare and sold her. After that Caretta bred several minor stakes winners.

I also bought for Mr. Jock Whitney for 24,000 guineas, the mare Aiming High, who won the Coronation Stakes for the Queen at Ascot in 1961. Of the same family as Caretta, Aiming High did him extremely well, breeding stakes winners including Ruritania and Family Doctor.

I was not so lucky for Jock Whitney when the 1966 King George VI and Queen Elizabeth Stakes winner Aunt Edith came up for sale privately at the end of that year. My partner Colonel Frank Beale was a friend of Colonel John Hornung, the owner, whose finances were struck a rude blow by the communists in Mozambique, who seized his sugar plantations. I told Frank Beale that any time he felt he had to sell the mare, I would do so in a week but that I would not worry him until he had made up his mind. Sometime later I heard on the grapevine that Aunt Edith had been sold. So Frank got on to Hornung and reminded him of his promise. He gave us forty-eight hours to sell the mare.

It was, through ill-luck, the time of an American bank holiday, which did not make it easier. I only mentioned her to two people. One of these was Jock Whitney, who said that he was "interested." I explained the time schedule but I do not think that he really understood the point, because he did not come back with a firm acceptance for several days. In the meantime, I was rung up by "Bull" Hancock, who said that he had already bought the mare. I told him that that was not what the owner had told me and that someone else had an option for forty-eight hours. "Bull" Hancock completed his purchase on behalf of Mr. Ogden Phipps, then Chairman of the New York Jockey Club, who boarded his mares with Hancock. Mr. Whitney was very upset about this. I think I underestimated the American understanding of the expression "I am interested" and he misunderstood what I had said about the urgency.

Some days later Richard Stanley rang me up and said that he was obliged to sell Waterloo, his home-bred winner of the 1972 1000 Guineas. Mr. Whitney's advisers did not think she was suitable probably because she was small and so I offered her to the ex-manager of our National Stud, Peter Burrell, who was by then married and resident in America. He knew the mare and accepted her at once. We have since seen several of her progeny race successfully here including Winter Frolic, a winner at Ascot in 1978 and Water Cay, a good two year old in 1985.

Another Oaks winner was offered to me for sale privately. This was Mrs. Stanhope Joel's 1970 Oaks winner Lupe; like Duke's Delight bred at the Joels' Snailwell Stud in Newmarket. Each man, as Oscar Wilde well knew, "kills the thing he loves" and the English Government is no exception, making it impossible to retain our greatest treasures such as works of art and top class mares and stallions, the seedcorn of bloodstock breeding. In this case a taxation problem made it necessary for the Joel family to sell something and Lupe had to go. I sold Lupe to Monsieur Wildenstein, who kept horses in France and America.

In all three cases these classic winners were not altogether lost to English racing, as progeny of all of them raced here and still do so. It was sad, however, that they had to go.

One of the results of past years of Socialist governments, sniping away at the capital of large scale stud owners, has been that our bigger individually owned studs have almost disappeared. One such case was when Lord Astor died in 1966 at the early age of 58. His death came at an awkward time for selling off his Cliveden Stud and the executors decided to make a sale by sealed bid. The BBA valued the stock for probate and were put in charge of the sealed bid sale. Because of our valuation we had an idea of the total value.

The sale of Lord Astor's mares and horses in training was widely advertised at home and abroad. It was after all one of the best and most successful band of brood-mares and race-horses in England. To our surprise there were few, if any serious inquiries, until Lord Rotherwick came along. He then had a few horses in training with Dick Hern and also owned a mare or two. The first filly he had bought for his stud was a foal by Petition out of the 1949 1000 Guineas and Oaks winner Musidora, whom I found for him at 6,100 guineas in 1960. Named Wishful Thinking she was a useful three-year-old and in due course a successful broodmare.

Nevertheless the acquisition of all Lord Astor's stock would give him at a stroke one of the most powerful stables and studs in the country. The idea appealed to him.

I could not tell Lord Rotherwick what to bid but I did give him an idea of what sort of figure would obtain them. I asked him to send in his bid in a sealed envelope so that I would not know what the figure was. Up to less than a week before the closing date his was the only bid received.

Then suddenly I had a telephone call from America saying that Mr. Bill Hackman from Middleburg, Virginia was interested and was coming over to see the stock. After seeing all he went away to decide on what to bid. I gave him the same rough figures as I had given Lord Rotherwick. The next day he came back with a firm bid and asked me if I thought he would get them. As far as I knew, Lord Rotherwick's was the only other firm bid received. I could only give him the same advice as to a possible figure but suggested that, if he wanted to be sure, he should increase his bid and send it in a sealed envelope direct, without showing it to me. I was then rung up by Lord Rotherwick's man of affairs, who said he hoped his Lordship was not making a fool of himself by bidding too much. I said that on the contrary he was probably not bidding quite enough and, if he really wanted to buy them, he should increase his bid, if only slightly. He did not heed my advice.

When the time came to open the envelopes, there were only two bids. They were within a few thousand or less of each other and Mr. Hackman had won. Lord Rotherwick was very upset, as was his wife.

However, I had an idea. I went to Bill Hackman and said "What are you going to do with the racehorses in the purchase? You can take the mares and foals and yearlings home and sell some at Saratoga if you like. But what about the racehorses? If I found a buyer for the lot, would you accept?" After a bit of thought, he said he would. I went back to Lord Rotherwick and said that I thought he could buy all the horses in Lord Astor's name in Dick Hern's stable. This should give him some fun while they raced and should produce a brood mare or two of value when they retired. He agreed and we came to a deal by which he bought the horses in training from Mr. Hackman, thus laying the foundation of Lord Rotherwick's Cornbury Stud at his home near Charlbury. It was a very weary Robin Hastings, who went to sleep that night!

As seems to be the case with most great dispersals, the stock did not greatly distinguish themselves in the new ownership. Bill Hackman sold his yearlings well and had one or two good fillies to race. But the results, though financially satisfactory, were not remarkable. Lord Rotherwick had fun with old Grey Of Falloden, who won a good race at Chester for him in 1967 and The Accuser, who won the Queen's Vase as a three-year-old in the same year and the Doncaster Cup as a four year old. Of the fillies he kept as broodmares, only Mitigation distinguished herself greatly as the dam of the Dee Stakes winner Colum, Conciliation and other winners,

Conciliation in due course being the dam of the good Morston horse Morcon, who ran well in Teenoso's Derby in 1983. Lord Rotherwick's best filly Swiftfoot, winner of the 1982 Irish Guinness Oaks, although tracing back to Lord Astor's blood, was not out of a mare bought at this time.

Looking back it is almost inconceivable that the great Astor collection should not have left a firmer impression on the bloodstock world of England and America, after his death.

CHAPTER 12

Saratoga

SARATOGA IS THE NAME to schoolboys which denotes the final surrender of the English redcoat forces to the American colonists. In another sense the Americans can now be said to have surrendered to the Arabs. The site of the second most important yearling sale in the States organised by the long established firm of Fasig Tipton, Saratoga grew up in the 19th century, first as a spa, where the water could be taken and baths of sulphur-like intensity used and secondly as a gambling hall for the New Yorkers on holiday. It is situated 150 miles or so north of New York, half way between the city and the Canadian border.

In order to amuse those taking the waters and as a relaxation from the gambling tables, two racecourses were built. You can now bet on flat races for nine races in the afternoon, grab a sandwich and then play up your winnings on nine trotting races in the evening. Many of the big stables bring their horses up for the six weeks of the summer season, when August in New York City would be too hot to endure.

It is fashionable to run some of the best two-year-olds for the first time at Saratoga and there are a number of "stakes" for all ages of nation-wide fame. Many of the big owners have summer houses in Saratoga. If you drive up the Broadway, there will be houses on either side of the road with spacious gardens and an "iron jockey", decked out in the colours of the Phipps, the Paysons, the Howell Jacksons — the great names of today and of a few years ago in American racing.

The Racing Museum has been established in Saratoga and for those who do not want to spend all their time with horses past and present, there are golf courses and the Performing Arts Centre, which features everything from the Boston

Philharmonic Orchestra to Shakespeare plays and jazz festivals. One of the attractions of Saratoga is supposed to be the climate. But I found it more humid than cool and sometime or other during my brief annual stay there were always some really hot days.

When Humphrey Finney of Fasig Tipton thought I was sufficiently attuned to the American way of life to be let loose at Saratoga, he invited me over for the sales in early August — between Goodwood and the grouse. For the first ten to fifteen years that I went there was no question of a foreigner buying a yearling except for an American. The power of the dollar, currency restrictions and economic stringency in Europe made sure of that. In those years an Englishman was a rarity; there was a scattering of Irishmen and a very few French and South Americans. The tide turned in the 1970's and now there are more Arabs, Europeans and South Americans than there are inhabitants of the States. That is for the sales week, the high point of the season.

At first I stayed in rooms — very hot and stuffy — then in the Reading Room, the club situated between the racecourse and the sales paddocks. There were three guest rooms, two with air conditioning. My fellow guests were E. P. Taylor and Captain Harry F. Guggenheim, for whom Sir Cecil Boyd-Rochfort trained with success in England. You can guess who had the room without any air conditioning — under the roof. Latterly I stayed at the Hotel Gideon Putman by courtesy of Danny and Peggy Van Clief, who normally provided me with a very large car and a chauffeur, Ben Paige, who drove me where I wanted. I was sometimes mistaken for a tycoon instead of a beggar!

Life during the sales week was at best somewhat hectic. A typical schedule is perhaps worth describing. It was advisable to be on the racetrack between six and seven in the morning to see the horses work and to visit the trainers in their barns. One of the best ports of call was Mr. Juck Whitney's house looking over his private barns on one side and his training track with the hills beyond. Alternatively I would often breakfast in the Reading Room where all present were poring over their racing programme in the *Morning Telegraph*. Then there were a couple or three hours to be spent at the sales paddocks, looking at yearlings.

Unlike England, where you are lucky to find anyone prepared to show you their wares, you have only to approach within a hundred yards of the box for a deputation to come up to you offering drinks, giving up-to-date details of relations of the beast and only too ready to pull him out for your inspection. The owner or his wife is generally sitting within earshot to note any remarks derogatory or otherwise — beware of loud criticism, or an exaggerated version will quickly reverberate round the sales paddocks!

After a hot hour or two, beating off the flies and looking at the yearlings it is time to change for lunch or a cocktail-party or both. This is followed by the races. I usually used to leave after the seventh race and spend another hour or so with the yearlings. Then there would be a cocktail party or dinner or both before the sales, which began at eight thirty and went on until midnight.

When I first went there, we solemnly changed into a dinner jacket before attending but that habit has lapsed. When the sales were finished there was a great temptation to linger in the little "pub" at the edge of the sales paddocks, which gloried in the name of The Spitin Divel. Two drinks there and it was next morning and only a few hours before you were down on "the track."

There were, of course, numerous parties, such as the Museum Ball which filled in any gaps in the programme and by the time the sales were over, there was always an early start to catch the plane — latterly Concorde — from New York. It took me a week or so to recover from Saratoga on my return home.

There were some more relaxing moments. It was impossible to find a better cook than Mr. & Mrs. Walter Jeffords had at their house. In the 1960's I always used to lunch with Mrs. Hope Iselin, a young lady of between 90 and 100. Like Captain Guggenheim she trained in England with Sir Cecil Boyd-Rochfort and when Cecil became unsound in his knees, we had an arrangement by which we saved him walking by going through a list of possible yearlings at Newmarket for Mrs. Iselin. For a fee, we at least discarded the cripples and he made his choice from the selections. One of these was Wolver Hollow and I remember standing next to Mrs. Iselin when he was engaged in a very close finish in the St. James's Palace Stakes at Ascot in 1967. Sadly, as her sight was now dim, she could not see the finish but she heard the result.

When I went to lunch with her at Saratoga, she always sat me on her right and after discussing weather, politics and the new elections to the Jockey Club, would say "Colonel Hastings, I hope you will not mind me talking business at luncheon. I want you to help Cecil buy a yearling or two for me." She thus reflected a set of manners of pre-war years.

For many years I could not bid for yearlings except for an occasional American with the dollars in his pocket. But I did find various clients for whom I had bought horses and inquired after their welfare and had always a few mares, foals and fillies to offer. As the times changed, more and more foreign buyers appeared and soon we were buying as much at Saratoga as at Newmarket.

In the year 1977 when the buying had begun, I was almost alone of my firm at the sales, except for Tom Cooper of BBA (Ireland). I had, as it happened, few orders and was outbid on several occasions on the first two days. Feeling that I was wasting my time, I went on looking at yearlings and came at last on something I really wanted. He was a bay colt, with black markings, a little white round three fetlocks, a quality but masculine head, strong neck, sloping shoulders, good forelegs, unless you thought him a trifle straight in front, well ribbed up, a good hind leg and strong hocks. He was rather flat over his quarters but then the dam was by Tom Rolfe, who inherited this trait from Ribot. He was a really good walker. He had "the look of eagles" but — and here was the crab — he was by Nijinsky. People like me do not normally get a look in at the progeny of that great horse.

Luckily his female line, though full of impeccably bred

mares and stallions, lacked the "black type," the list of stake races won, which are generally associated with a son of Nijinsky. He did however go back to Winkle, a mare sent out to Admiral Grayson's stud in Virginia many years ago by the BBA, as I have already recorded.

I could not take my eyes off the horse. Eventually I plucked up the courage to ring up Lady Beaverbrook. When her racing manager, Sir Gordon Richards, was on the verge of retirement and her manager Mr. Bob Crowhurst was still working with Reynolds, Leader and Day, the Newmarket vets, we had done some business with her. In fact, I had bought her a yearling in Ireland who won at Royal Ascot. Now with her trainers, vet and manager all an ocean away it was up to me.

I must have infected Lady Beaverbrook with some of my enthusiasm, because she was interested at once. But Nijinsky spelt money and I did not want to land her in one of those duels with the Arabs and Robert Sangster which go on all night. She told me — bravely — to go ahead. My bid was to be about a quarter of what I thought he would fetch; at least I had no explicit limit. But I was determined not to go mad and to set my own limit at a reasonable sum.

I asked Tom Cooper to confirm my judgement and he gave qualified approval only — which made me fairly sure that Robert Sangster would not be interested.

On the night of the sale, I went to a particularly good dinner-party where I was well-placed. It came to my mind to stay on there and not have the mortification of seeing the horse go beyond my price. But luckily I did not!

There was, in fact, little interest in the yearling round the ring. I bought him for 90,000 dollars, which I guessed to be somewhere near the reserve.

Lady Beaverbrook was pleased. But then our troubles began. He was put on an aeroplane bound for Heathrow and while in mid-air, a strike of air controllers broke out, so that he was diverted to Germany. There he was not only not allowed to leave the plane but not provided with suitable food and water. After forty-eight hours we got permission to take him on to England. He arrived in a badly dehydrated state at Sir John Astor's stud at Newmarket, where Aitken, the stud groom, was not greatly impressed with him on arrival. But he did a magnificent job on him and got him in good enough health to go into training with Dick Hern, though later than I would have liked. Then he pulled a muscle behind, so that he only had one educational run as a two-year-old.

The next year I was at Newmarket on 1000 Guineas day and noticed that a three-year-old by Nijinsky out of Virginia Hills called Niniski was due to run over a mile appropriately perhaps in the Hastings Stakes. This was the horse. I am glad to say that he won cleverly. From then on he improved and in all won five group races. His worst race was in the 200th Derby, won by Troy. It came too soon for him and he finished ninth of 23. He disappointed also in the St. Leger, in which he was joint favourite, after an impressive success at Newbury in August. Willie Carson told me later that, if the St. Leger was re-run, he would have won. He had great speed for one short run and held up at Doncaster for another furlong, Willie felt that he would have beaten the two French out-and-out stayers Son Of Love and Soleil Noir who beat him into third place.

Niniski then went on to win first the Irish St Leger by ten lengths at the Curragh and a fortnight later the Prix Royal Oak — the French St Leger at Longchamp — both on soft going.

As a four-year-old, Niniski started well enough but managed to get beaten in the Coronation Cup on very hard going, and never regained his form. Months afterwards when at stud, he developed a corn very high up which necessitated an operation. Probably this corn, quite undetectable at that stage, is what stopped him on the hard going.

Here now was a horse by Nijinsky from an excellent female line, good looking, the winner of five group races, two of them Group 1. You would have thought there would have been a rush of people wanting to buy shares. But no : the word stayer frightened them off.

130

However, Miss Kirsten Rausing, who had come from Sweden to buy the Lanwades Stud, summed up the situation and asked if she could buy into the horse. Lady Beaverbrook let her have ten shares and the horse was put on the market for syndication of a limited number of shares. There was no rush to buy. After an interval Lady Beaverbrook closed the syndication, retaining a fair proportion of shares herself. Though some people were turned down, it could not be said that the horse was over subscribed. Nor was there a rush for his nominations. His first season of runners was to change all that.

During the summer of 1983, we were, of course, looking round for yearlings. Unless you are in the million guineas mark, you have to consider first season stallions. There were two yearlings at Miss Rausing's Lanwades stud, one was out of a grey mare belonging to an Italian, who had fallen on bad times — at least he would not pay for fees or keep. Kirsten Rausing went to court and obtained permission to sell the grey mare Kalazero and her Niniski yearling at Tattersalls Newmarket July Sales. She bought the yearling for 7,200 guineas. At that point, he was a rather backward colt with "open" knees. By the time she put him in the autumn yearling sales, he had improved and was bought by the BBA for Mr. Ravi Tikkoo for only 11,000 guineas. He was named Kala Dancer and, as is well-known, he won his two races at two, the second being the 1984 Group 1 Dewhurst Stakes, only to break a blood vessel probably as a result of a virus at three years. He was then sent out to race in California.

The other colt was a bay from the family of Val De Loir. From a foal, he was an imposing individual, not easy to fault. I saw him two or three times at Lanwades and suggested to Lady Beaverbrook that she should buy him, as she had not another Niniski yearling of her own breeding. She and Bob Crowhurst went out to see him at Lanwades. The meeting was a great success. They both liked the colt. He was by a first season horse out of a mare as yet unproven at stud. You would be buying his looks. I had no definite instructions as to a limit but I knew Lady Beaverbrook wanted him enough to pay rather more than the average for a colt by Niniski, which anyway was not yet established.

When the colt came into the ring, I was thinking of somewhere between 25,000 and 50,000 guineas. It was soon obvious that he was going for a good deal more. I was just thinking that the auctioneer was talking to himself — that is going up to the reserve — when I noticed that Geoffrey Wragg and Sir Philip Oppenheimer were nodding their heads. So eventually I decided to "come in" and was much relieved to see the hammer fall to my nod at 90,000 guineas. I was afraid I would get in trouble for paying too much but Lady Beaverbrook took it well and told me to arrange for the colt to go to Dick Hern. Once again this was a relief as I knew that Dick liked him.

Only two or three times in the thirty-three years I was with the BBA has a trainer said straight away that a horse is a good one. Dick Hern never thought Petoski was anything else but top-class. He was not taken in by the general idea that Niniski would get slow stayers. He got Petoski ready to have a run at Royal Ascot but that was a year when the going was hard; so he put off his first appearance until the Champagne Stakes at Salisbury at the end of June.

I was not able to go but I understand that Dick Hern said to Willie Carson "I have been training this horse to be a good staying horse. I have not been jumping him off, but letting him find his stride and go up to the others in the last furlong. Ride him like that today, please."

I understand that Lady Beaverbrook said "Carson, I have come all the way from Newmarket. I want you to win!" Willie Carson touched his cap and did exactly as they both said. He let him idle out of the gate and come through in the last furlong to win impressively. The next time out, ridden by Joe Mercer, he won the Lanson Champagne Stakes at Goodwood, not very easily. But it was a good performance by a horse trained to be a three-year-old against Provideo who was the opposite and was the winner of thirteen races that season.

After the Lanson Champagne at Goodwood came the

Laurent Perrier Champagne Stakes at Doncaster, where Petoksi had a very bad run and was a fast finishing third. In his final race as a two-year-old in the Royal Lodge Stakes at Ascot, different tactics were pursued, but after leading into the straight, Petoksi dropped right out. He was probably "over the top".

During the winter Dick Hern had his hunting accident and an unkind fate decreed that as he was recovering his horses should have a strange virus. They looked well, jumped and kicked at exercise, ran well in their races until the last furlong when they packed up and blew a great deal. Early on at Sandown, Petoski ran Damister, a future Derby third, to a length over 1¼ miles in the Guardian Classic Trial. At Chester, where he got into trouble on the final turn and then had to pull round Piggott's mount Miller's Mate who had split a pastern, he was second to Law Society, the future Irish Derby winner, who in his next race after Chester was second to Slip Anchor in the Derby, before going on to win the Irish Derby.

Then Petoski had another misfortune. He came out in spots all over his coat — not ringworm but possibly the after-effects of the stable's virus. It was only just possible to get him ready or half-ready to run in the Derby: there is only one Derby every year. In the race he showed speed and lasted until they were round Tattenham Corner but then gradually dropped back. Willie Carson was not hard on him when he saw he could not be placed.

Dick Hern then wisely put him away until he showed him that he was really well again. Like everyone else he could not be sure that he really had a top-class horse. Perhaps he did not stay. He toyed with the idea of keeping him for the Scottish Derby, a pale shadow of the Epsom race. Lady Beaverbrook, however, had not given up hope and preferred to run in the Princess of Wales's Stakes over one and a half miles at the Newmarket July Meeting.

By the time he arrived at Newmarket he looked a picture of health. In the race he showed a return to his best form and, although shut in on the rails at one moment, he came round

133

his opponents and won easily, with his lovely action making a fine sight as he galloped up the hill to the winning post.

The Scottish Derby looked at his mercy. But bravely his connections decided to try a little higher and declared him for the King George VI and the Queen Elizabeth Diamond Stakes at Ascot. The opposition included the Prix de l'Arc de Triomphe winner Rainbow Quest, the Irish Oaks winner Princess Patti and the Australian bred Strawberry Road, the best of the older horses. The favourite was the three-year-old Oh So Sharp, winner of the 1000 Guineas and the Oaks, and his old rival Law Society. The only notable absentees were the Derby winner Slip Anchor, who was on the easy list, and the Eclipse winner Pebbles. It was a very distinguished field of twelve.

The race was run at a very fast pace on fast going. Coming to the turn for home Willie Carson was well behind, conserving the sharp burst of speed which Petoski and Niniski shared. Coming into the straight he got a fairly hefty bump from something dropping back beaten and well into the straight it looked as if he would be pinned against the rails and would not get out in time to make a challenge. But the gap came, Willie Carson pulled to the outside and coming with a really powerful run he won " going away " in my view by a neck from Oh So Sharp with Rainbow Quest three quarters of a length further away third and Law Society fourth.

On that day Petoski was the best horse in Europe. He had avenged the defeat of Lady Beaverbrook's Bustino by Grundy in the same race ten years before and he had shown how adversity had not blunted the skill of his trainer.

The programme for the rest of the season was to include the St Leger but an injury behind prevented him from running again as a three-year-old.

Though Petoski remained in training for the 1986 season, he never recaptured his form of July 1985 and was retired to the National Stud. I had no such luck and retired to my home, where I could at last pay due attention to my wife and my dogs, who had been so sadly neglected during my business life.

134

Looking Back

INFLATION HAS BEEN the biggest factor. Prices of yearlings, stallion fees and training fees have all escalated and the traditional English owner breeder has almost become a thing of the past. Apart from Her Majesty The Queen, Lord Howard de Walden and Mr. Robert Sangster, there are, since Mr. Jim Joel's dispersal, few large private studs in the hands of English owners. There are several large commercial studs, standing stallions and selling yearlings, but the English owner of sixteen mares is now a rarity.

In their place the Arabs, Greeks, Americans and Chinese have taken over. If you go round Newmarket to visit the famous studs, you will find that almost all have passed in the last few years into the hands of foreigners. The Arab influx is a great thing for England and English racing. It is perhaps a pity that the first three in a maiden two-year-old race at Pontefract are likely to be all Arab-owned and dearly bought. But it must be faced that such are the costs of racing and breeding that it is a hobby which few Englishmen can now afford on a large scale.

If I was asked to recall the best-looking horses I had met, I should go back a long way, not so much for fear of contradiction, but because they stand out in my mind. Bahram would be my ideal type of flat race horse, standing, I suppose, about 15.3 hh with a lovely head and eye, an Arab neck and beautifully symmetrical. I saw his Derby and years afterwards a group of mares by him in Argentina, all stamped with his quality. Of the jumpers Kellsborough Jack stands out and Sir Alfred Munnings has in no way flattered him by showing him as a picture of perfectly balanced symmetrical beauty.

Talking of symmetry you would find it hard to beat

135

Nearco. Again not a big horse, every part of him was perfectly aligned to the rest. He was an old horse by the time I knew him and a great character with his private air raid shelter and his habit of putting out his tongue.

Never Too Late was my favourite filly; again she was small but beautifully balanced and a great mover. To see her come round Tattenham Corner well in the rear and run through the whole Oaks field to win easily was a sight to remember.

The best looking horses or the most correctly made are not always the best racehorses. But there is nearly always a reason for a horse being a disappointment or a "dog", something very likely which will not be apparent until they are dead. I once rode a horse for Peter Cazalet, who had his sights set on the Grand Military, as he belonged to a soldier. I rode him at Kempton on the day after Boxing Day. He had won a good-class novice chase the time before and so we were odds on. He gave me a terrible ride, missing every second fence, taking off anywhere and only just in touch coming to the last. He made a mess of that and by the time I had collected him and myself, he still had enough class to get up and win.

Peter Cazalet was mystified and decided he was better when fresh so that he did not run again until the Sandown race in March. There he looked marvellous but after one circuit started to root them and at the third of the fences on the far side managed to dislodge me. The owner was furious. He kept him in training and two years later, I was surprised to be rung up by Fulke Walwyn asking me to ride him in the Grand Military. As happened at the beginning of most March's I had broken my collar-bone at Cheltenham and could not ride. He ran a fair race and was, I think, fourth. Shortly afterwards, he died and the post mortem showed that he had the smallest heart for a horse his size that the vet had ever seen. But he could not tell us why he sometimes could not perform.

Perfect looks do not always mean success at stud nor the other way round. I inspected a horse of Lord Rosebery's once called Copenhagen. He was a nice chestnut horse with an arch to his neck, good limbs and quality all through. But when he walked towards you, he did not walk straight. I cabled out an exact description and to my surprise our clients bought him. When I went to New Zealand two years afterwards, I went in fear and trembling to the stud where he stood, expecting a stern lecture on the facts of horse conformation from the owner. Not a bit of it, they were delighted with him, though he still was not a straight mover. They were right to like him. He was champion sire in New Zealand at least twice.

Every year it is clearly proved that no-one can accurately forecast whether a horse is going to be a success at stud or not. If you are buying for someone abroad, you can only stick to one rule and that is the horse should be as correct as possible. At one time I used to rush to the unsaddling enclosure after big races and try to calculate why the winner was a good horse. There was only one common factor which applies to practically all good racehorses. They all have plenty of heart room from withers to elbow. I remember seeing the great Tulloch after winning in Melbourne and finding that the only point in conformation that stood out was depth from withers to elbow. I suppose that was what appealed to Tommy Smith when he bought him.

On the other hand, some horses with definite faults do not reproduce them. I am inclined to think that you can often get away with bad hocks, which may be the result of a mishap in foaling and not of heredity. Nobody could claim that Vaigly Great or Sharpo have correct hocks and yet look how well they have both done. Looks are not everything. It would be a long shot if the five most expensive yearlings of 1986 proved to be the best racehorses of 1987.

If I had to choose from all the horses I have ridden, looked at and bid for, bought or sold, those which gave me the greatest pleasure, I would put up two. One was Apricot, who apart from running away with Charlie Smirke, managed to carry me round successfully in three hurdle races. The other is Fenny Rough, who won three times in the colours of my wife, Jean, the last time in the Oak Tree Stakes at Goodwood, illustrating to me — usually a mere onlooker — the thrill of owning and winning with your own horse.

Freddie Maxwell used to say he could not see racing coming to an end. "After all, when a man is over forty he begins to feel he is not so good in bed; he knows he does not go so well out hunting, and more and more pheasants manage to fly by unscathed — so what else is there left to do but own a racehorse?"

Index

140

142

144

Nearco

at the sta

Peter B

Hydroplane